THE MODERN GOLD TRADING SYSTEM:
A NEW VISION FOR INVESTORS

By
Paul R. Hamilton

ISBN: 1490954538
ISBN 13: 9781490954530
Library of Congress Control Number: 2013912599
CreateSpace Independent Publishing Platform
North Charleston, South Carolina

This book is dedicated to my Dad, Donald A. Hamilton who recently passed (1922-2012). He was a 30 year US Navy veteran of three wars who was a great man and wonderful Dad.

For the men of science who taught me to love the world of numbers. Thank you, Dr. Richard Hill, Dr. Brad Lashbrook and Dr. James C McCroskey.

For Jack Mauch who always keeps me pointed in the right direction.

For my fellow alumni and former teachers around the world. To all Kodiak High School Bears (63), Long Beach City College Vikings (AA), California State University at Long Beach 49ers (BA) and Illinois State University Cardinals (MS) You didn't make me a better student but a more imaginative thinker.

Table of Contents

INTRODUCTION

Systems

As humans, we are surrounded by a world of systems. We live, work and play in a diverse universe of systems every day. Most Americans don't give it much thought. Some don't care. When it comes to investing, learning about how systems interact may be the most important lesson in your life.

A generic definition of a system is a set of things that are all connected to form a whole unit. Almost all systems have four characteristics. They are structure, behavior, interconnectedness, and function. I don't claim to be a big maven when it comes to systems. I took a graduate seminar on cybernetics as part of my PhD program at the University of Oregon. I hated that course with a burning passion and could not wait for it to end so I could make my escape down 11ᵗʰ street to Duffy's tavern. I got a B which is the kiss of death in any graduate program. To be clear, I am a MS and not a PhD.

While I hated the course, I loved systems analysis. I know what a system looks like and in 1988, I began to concentrate on computer behavior and the markets with gusto. It wasn't long before I had a clear idea how all the parts of the S&P 500 interacted with one another. Ten years later in 1998, I decided to study gold.

I had one of those rare flash of a bright light moment while reading the *Wall Street Journal*. For whatever reason, I decided to start with the gold futures and follow their influence throughout all the diverse parts of the different gold investments. I started with the gold futures and followed it to the end of the chain, options. I now had a clear vision of the gold market trading system. I should have seen it all a lot sooner. I knew there had been a seismic change in the stock market back in the early 1980's. Volume mushroomed from maybe seven million shares a day to more than one hundred million shares a day. A market that struggled to get to 1,000 was blasting to 2,000 like a bat out of hell. Something had changed?

The Revolution of August 18th, 1982: The Rise of the Machines

During the decade of the 1970's, computers were information slaves for the financial services industry. They held vast amounts of data about corporations and customer's accounts. That was about all they did. Passive players in the game of investing. Computers did not have a hand in any decision making or the execution of trades. They were deaf, dumb and docile.

In the 1980's, all that began to change. On August 18th, 1982, a bloodless revolution happened. The computers, nothing more than electro-mechanical machines, overtook the humans in the trading of stocks. By now, the machines began to make investment decisions and execute trades without any human input. August 18th, 1982 was the first 100 million share day on the NYSE. Such an event would have been totally impossible without computerized trading. To put this monumental event into its proper context, consider this, the first one million share day was December 15th, 1886. It took nearly 100 years for the volume to increase by a factor of 100. It would take a mere fifteen years for NYSE volume to balloon to one billion shares, October 27th,1997. Astonishingly, it would take less than a decade, eight short years, for the NYSE crack the three billion share mark, June 24th, 2005. None of this would have been possible without computerized trading. Bigger computers, more speed, the explosion of derivatives and the addition of ETFs would all contribute to this phenomenal growth spurt. Computerized trading would also be known as robo trading, algorithmic trading, or black box trading. Almost from the beginning, investors would come to mistrust and hate the machines.

I was at first curious and then fell in love with the computers. A new mistress had entered my life. The first computer trades were between the index futures and index funds of the S&P 500. It wasn't long before the machines were trading all manner of equities. All you needed was an index fund and index futures.

Today, it would almost be easier to construct a list of investments that are not traded by computers than those that are. The vast panorama of the computerized world of investments can be found on the NYSE Arca exchange. It is breath taking in size and scope. The web of computerized investments encompass the entire planet.

One thing is for sure, a 100% bet. Computerized trading is our past, present, and future. It is a part of your reality. The sooner you learn to embrace the computers, the happier you will be. The quicker you learn how to read these systems the faster you will be able to exploit them.

Investing: Humans Versus Machines

The only commonality between human and machine investing today is they both trade stocks, bonds and derivatives. After that, the differences are sharp, distinct, and stark. Cat and dog different. Night and day different. Men are from Mars, women are from Venus different. They are, in fact, polar opposites.

Investing Differences Between Humans and Machines

Humans	Machines
single investment strategy	multiple investment strategies
buy long	buy long and short
buy and hold	buy and sell
buy low-sell high	buy high-sell higher
based on analysis (fundamental/technical)	based on recognition
based on earnings	based on price alone
holds on to losers	quickly sells losers
emotion based (greed/fear)	computer logic based
based on sales hype	based solely on facts (price)
contra trend buyers	trend buyers
high risk behavior	low risk behavior
inception date: 1934 (79 years)	1982 (31 years)

We could debate the merits of each side until the Holsteins come home. The real question for you to ponder is which one makes the most money?

When it comes to profits, the computers are the clear winners over humans by a country mile. While algorithmic traders do not post their earnings, there are some clear signals, they are money making machines. M. Narang of Tradewerks told Steve Kroft of CBS 60 Minutes, " We've had two or three days in a row where we lost. But we've never had a week, so far, where we lost. We've never had a month that was a loser for us." Given the fact that Tradwerks trades 40 million shares a day that is a fantastic trade record. How happy would you be with a winning record like this?

According to Joe Saluzzi of Themis Trading LLC, "There was even one firm that said they made money four years in a row every single day." While here say is a low level of evidence, this is a fascinating story that bends the laws of probability. What if all this were true?

We do know that HFTs made $21 billion in profits in 2008 during one of histories worst market meltdowns. While small investors were being financially crucified, machine traders were swimming in profits. Don't you wish you could have banked profits in 2008?

As far as I can see, there has never been an algorithmic firm turn to the public for financing with an IPO. Since 1982, the number of listed firms equals ZERO! They don't need our money to make money.

How to Win Like the Computers

The only way to win like the computers is to change your attitude from being a victim to that of a victor. From chump to champ. From helpless loser to self confidant winner. This may be easier said than done. As a college instructor teaching persuasion (attitude change), I know it is a scientific fact that it is very tough changing attitudes that are cast in concrete. The more deeply held an attitude, the harder it is to change. If you can't keep an open mind about using data based computer behavior then this book probably won't work for you.

Rage against the machines runs deep. In a poll, 90% of the respondents saw the market as "unfair" to small investors. Fifty percent of the investors had little or zero confidence in the ability of regulators to make the market fair for every investor. A puny 8% expressed a high level of confidence in regulators. The vast majority felt less confident in buying individual stocks and blamed market volatility for their feelings. That's too bad, for with great volatility, comes great wealth opportunities.

Finally, there is a faint glimmer of hope. In the poll, 38% of investors didn't really have an attitude about computerized trading one way or the other. A surprising 35% saw it as good to positive. Those attitudes about computerized trading may not being held hostage in a deep, dark, concrete bunker after all.

Human feelings of anger and helplessness can be traced all the way back to the early 1980's. We tend to fear what we don't understand. For small investors, computerized trading was a secret shrouded in darkness. They were fed the standard party line that computer program trading consisted of buying/ selling a basket of 15 stocks worth at least $1 million. The goal was to capture small price differences between the S&P Index Futures and the S&P 500 Index Funds. Even today, small investors, are told the benefits to them were increased liquidity and lower transaction costs. It's all nothing more than a 800 pound red herring!

The big lie behind the whole idea was that price differences between the futures and indexes happened naturally. You need to burn this into your brain. **The strategy behind all computerized trading is to manipulate one part of the system to provoke a predictable response in other components of the system.** Can you show me how? For example, a computer could short the S&P 500 stocks, the futures, the index funds, go long puts, and then sell the S&P100. This would drive the S&P 500 stocks, the futures and the index funds down while driving the puts up. Bingo, instant profits. On the flip side, a computer could buy a long position in the S&P 500 stocks, the futures, the index funds while going long the calls then buy the Major Market Index (XMI) or the Dow 30. Every part of the system goes up. Very smart and extremely lucrative.

The goal of all computerized trading, past and present, is to create a risk less trade. While Wall Street markets massive unknown risk to it's clients, they have very little risk tolerance with their own money.

The system was far from perfect and events of October 1987 would show that Wall Street had unseen risk built into the system. I can sum up the entire disaster in a single sentence. In 1987, two computer programs went to war with each other and both sides lost. It was computerized program trading versus portfolio insurance. In the end, it was an act of cyber cannibalism where the system began to feed on itself.

While academics would endlessly debate October 1987 over coffee, the best explanation was the Brady Report: Presidential Task Force on Market Mechanisms (1988). I read this report so many times, the words melted away to be replaced by a schematic diagram of the whole system locked inside my head.

In 2007, the black box traders would evolve with the introduction of High Frequency Trading, HFT where stocks were bought and sold within tiny fractions of a second. Program traders could stampede the market up or down and HFTs then cherry picked winners with micro second trades. If investors hated program trading, they despised HFT with a passion.

In 2010, the investment world was rocked when the Dow 30 fell a gut wrenching 1,000 points in a 30 minute free fall. Some lame brain trader for a mutual fund entered a $5 billion market order into the system. HFTs began to over load the system with almost simultaneous buy orders with simultaneous orders to cancel the trades. The machines suffered from what I call "computer psychosis" where some stocks plummeted to a penny a share while others jumped to $100 a share without any apparent reasons. The event known as the "flash crash" would damage investor psyche's far more than October 1987.

Louise Pollard spoke for millions when she remarked, " at this point, I would not want to get back into individual stocks. I don't have any confidence in the stock market, to be honest. It's just a gut feeling." Investors would vote with their check books and dump $288 billion in stock mutual funds into mutual fund bond funds. Investors would sell individual stocks in a raging bull market for the safe harbor of computer traded bonds. They jumped out of the fire into the frying pan.

As investors fled the system, the influence of the black box operators grew exponentially. Individual participation in the stock market would hover around the ten per cent level. Ditto for options. HFTs, who represent a miniscule 2% or just 400 out of 20,000 investment firms, were generating 73% of the trades on Wall Street. I believe the human component could disappear from the system and the machines would continue to function without missing a beat.

The 400 HFT firms are largely unknown to the public. I can only name a bakers dozen. They are, however, well known in Washington DC as campaign donation big hitters. Everything they do is 100% legal. Their power radiates from Constitution Avenue in DC not on Wall Street in NYC. As systems grow larger, more complex, and more exotic, they become fragile and prone to breakdowns. These breakdowns are a constant worry for small investors. Wall Street plays them down by calling them "glitches." For Wall Street to call them "glitches" is like saying the sinking of the RMS Titanic was a "boating accident." They are, more accurately, system failures. If the press called them system failures, the blood pressure of the average investor would jump 20 points!

2012 would give birth to two major league "glitches": Knight Capital Group's mini-flash-crash and NASDAQ's botched Facebook (FB) IPO. Knight Capital suffered a $400 million trading loss when an old software glitch multiplied orders by 1,000! As the American philosopher, Forrest Gump once said, "stupid is as stupid does." The real scary issue here is anyone can plug anything, like an untested program, into the system. A system without stringent quality controls is just cruising for a bruising. Someday, every monitor screen around the world will go blank, because some jerk nerd goofed up.

NASDAQ was fined $10 million, the largest ever charged to an exchange for it's botched handling of Facebook's (FB) IPO. Initial trading was delayed and buyers faced long wait times to find out if their orders were executed. More than 30,000 FB orders were held hostage in the NASDAQ system for more than two hours. The issue was a programming failure that was supposed to match buy/sell IPO orders. A programming band aid fix failed and the result was trading chaos.

These "glitches" are mostly software and programming foul ups where firms have shot themselves in the foot. Hardware issues seem nearly non existent. How bad is the problem of "glitches" and should I be worried? If you divided the number of "glitches" by the total number of executed trades, the result would be incredibly tiny. So small, that rather than obsessing with night terrors of the "glitch monster," you should sleep soundly tonight.

When it comes to investing, there is a need for speed. Modern computers are so fast, there are no words to describe how quick they are. If you were to take just one single second, chop it into a million pieces, that's how computers count time. Count just two of those million pieces and that's how fast the Dow Jones beat it's competitors in breaking a news story about interest rates. Count 48 of those million pieces and that's how long it takes to execute a trade. That's an amazing 21,000 trades in just one single second. When compared to humans, we are the tortoise and the machines are the hare. Memory capacity for today's computers are so immense, you can't imagine how big they are. Watson, the IBM super computer, who whipped one of my hero's, all time Jeopardy! Champ, Ken Jennings, contained a 15 terabyte data bank of knowledge. One terabyte (TB) is 1,000,000,000,000 bytes of information. That equals 1,000 copies of an encyclopedia.

Most humans have a memory capacity of 3 terabytes. Ken Jennings was facing a rigged game where humans were guaranteed a second place finish. Interestingly, Watson, Big Blue's champ isn't the biggest computer brain in IBM's world. Somewhere, IBM has a 128 TB, monster super computer. Who do you want investment data from, a super computer or a human? When compared to the 128 TB colossus, a human has the memory capacity of a very small rodent- a mouse!

On Wall Street, every second or fraction of a second, is for sale to the highest bidder and they aren't cheap. For a fee, HFTs, can get a 2 second sneak peak at pending trades and economic reports.

For news reports, it's called "event jumping" and it's all perfectly legal. At least one legal eagle doesn't think it's fair. Richard Painter, former Republican

White House ethics lawyer calls this a "blind spot" in US law. Painter feels that groups should "not be allowed to selectively market moving data to people who pay more money-that's not right." Easy for Painter to say, he isn't running for public office and doesn't need any Wall Street campaign loot.

Algorithmic traders using "machine readable news" can analyze and execute trades in a fraction of a second. On March 15,2013, stocks tumbled on an University of Michigan report that consumer confidence was lower than expected. Infinium Capital using a 2 second first look at the report was able to analyze the report and trade 7 million shares short in just one second. It was like shooting Dolly Varden trout in a barrel.

A human, any human, would go insane trying to make a constant millisecond decisions. It's a case of stimulus over load. You should forget about being a fraction of a second trader. Split second trades are not and probably never will be a part of your investment experience. Thank God for small favors. Day trading was bad enough, split second trading would be a human disaster!

The key to using computer behavior or data collection (they are the same), to your favor is to turn your attention to longer term computer behavior. If you do, there's a whole new investment world in your future. If you were to seek just two bytes of information a day, you will always know the market's trend. You will never be surprised by a bear market or miss the rewards of a bull market. If you were to seek just three bytes of information once a week for stocks and ETFs, then you can control your own investment future without any outside influences. There will only be that little voice inside your head controlling your investment behavior in bear or bull markets.

Think Like a Human, Act Like a Computer

It's a fact, we can't make decisions as fast as a computer and our memory banks can't hold as much information. What behavior can we possibly mimic from computers that would make us better investors? If you want to win like a computer, you need to imitate their behavior in three ways. First, when making all investment buy/sell decisions, concentrate solely on only one variable, price. Second, never ever fight the tape. After all, the trend is truly your best friend. Finally, learn how to win big in bear markets.

I wonder if it has ever crossed your mind why Wall Street doesn't do a better job of making money for investors? After all, they have access to mountains of data, top notch human brain power, unlimited use of main frame computers and tons of money? The answer is much simpler than you think. Wall Street for all its trappings, doesn't have a clue what a winner looks like! It's called paralysis by analysis.

Out of all the billions of numbers that cross the tape every day, the computers knows which ones are winners and buys them. You want to know the secret of computers and making money? For the most part, computers buy winners and avoids losers. Humans buy losers and avoid winners. In the case of computer buying behavior, they pick winners by the process of recognition. Wall Street depends on a complex, multi variable process of trying to find winners. Computers know what a winner looks like and hunts them down with ruthless efficiency. The humans rely on a horribly complex process and the machines opt for a simple single variable course of action.

Imagine how serene your world would be if you could tell if a stock, ETF, index fund, or futures contract was a buy or sell simply by just glancing at its price? **Winners are identified by the machines exclusively by price alone**. If you want to master this skill, there's a single assumption that you must go all in. You need to believe that all the available news is reflected in the current price. Since we know that computers are hooked up to news feeds and trade in micro seconds, this is a very safe assumption. External forces are always a part of the investment process. Good news like positive earnings, bumps up in analysts ratings, and low interest rates send the markets up. Bad news like earnings that miss the mark, analysts down grades and higher interest rates send the markets down. It isn't as easy as it sounds.

Every deck of cards has two jokers and using price exclusively as your buy/sell signals are no different. The one element that no one controls, human or machine, are life's unpredictable, out of left field, world wide events. Only someone from Wall Street would call the horrible events of 9-11 a "non linear random event." I prefer calling them the jokers in the deck. The reason, black box traders invest for a fraction of a second is they know, time is always their biggest risk. For them, less holding time means, the chance of fewer jokers.

There's an added benefit to solely using price to make investment decisions that probably never crossed your mind. At some point, you can match the price to the situation where it appeared. After that, you can assign a win-loss percentage. Ask your broker what are the chances your purchase will go up or down and all you'll get is a blank stare. For the first time, you an adjust your risk appetite before you invest. If a 50/50 investment is too low, you just have to wait for a more favorable bet.

Let's end this with a sports analogy. I love baseball, particularly when the play offs and the World Series rolls around. Every hitter worth his salt knows to get a hit,you have to shut out all distractions and concentrate on seeing the ball. For investors, the price is the ball. If you keep your eye on the ball then you'll more likely get hit than to strike out. The ball is everything. Price is everything. Computers are NEVER contrarian investors. They NEVER trade against the trend or contra to the business cycle. Only humans try to out guess the markets and they pay the price with hefty losses.

For black box traders, the trend is not only their friend, but their bosom buddy. They are attached to each other. Of all the strategies the computers use to squeeze a nickel out of the system, trend investing is the only one that humans can mimic. While computers have unlimited access to data, all you need is Yahoo! Finance and the <u>Wall Street Journal</u> to master the trend.

Wall Street is expert at manufacturing mountains of words and the following is their party line about computers and trend investing.

> "Trend investing is an investment strategy that tries to take advantage of long term, medium term and short term movements that occur in various markets. The strategy aims to take advantage on both sides, going long (buying) or short (selling) in an attempt to profit from the ups and downs of the stock or futures market. Traders initiate a trade when the trend appears to have started and exit once the trend appears to have ended."
>
> (84 words)

What's all this mean and how do I fit in? Try this on for size. In a bull market, the computers buy the upticks, advances, and 52 week highs. In a bear market, the computers sell the down ticks, declines, and 52 week lows.(30 words) Tell me more? Buying begets more buying, trends gain traction and morph into bull markets. For ALL classes of investments there is a concert of new 52 week highs in ALL the components of the long positions. In a bull market, the short ETF will trade to new 52 week lows. Calls are the only choice for a responsible options players concentrating on the long new 52 week highs. Puts are recommended for the short side ETF making new 52 week lows. Stocks, bonds, commodities, or currencies, this is the way all the systems work.

Selling fathers more selling and down trends gain momentum and transform themselves into bear markets. For ALL classes of investments in a bear market there is a concert of new 52 week lows in ALL components of the long positions. The short ETF will trade to new 52 week highs. Puts are the only choice for responsible option investors. Put buyers need to focus on components making new 52 week lows. Calls are the only choice for inverse ETFs making new 52 week highs. Stocks, bonds, commodities, and currencies, this is the way the systems work. There is no deviation in computer behavior across all systems. None, zilch, nada,zero!

Contrary to what you think, there's an easy way to know when a trend begins. So simple, a computer literate teenager could master it. Where the trend ends is a tad bit murkier. The one thing that I admire most about black box traders is their ability to ring up huge profits in a bear market. If you were to reject everything else and learn this one skill, I would be the happiest man on earth!

The key to understanding how to win big in bear markets comes from knowing about the world of ETFs. Investor complaints about ETFs tend to cluster around two points. First, investors feel there are too many ETFs and they don't know which ETFs they should own. The first complaint is easy to fix. If you follow a small universe of ETFs, you can ignore the rest. If you are not interested in copper, natural gas, sugar, China, muni bonds, or real estate, don't waste your time window shopping. Which ETFs to own is as simple as one-two. I never, ever just watch one, single ETF at a time. I always study matched pairs of ETFs. Currently, I follow the following matched pairs: DDM v DXD, DUST v NUGT, UGLD v DGLD, ULE v EUO, YCL v YCS, PSQ v QQQ, RWM v UWM, SCO v UCO, USLV v DSLV, SPXU v UPRO and TBT v UBT. Next year, I intend to add YINN v YANG and possibly a matched pair following natural gas.

You look both ways before crossing the street, why not look both ways before you invest? When one of the matched pairs goes up, the other goes down about 98% of the time. You don't need a MBA degree from some big time university to know you want to own the one going up.

In a way, I don't think ETFs were ever intended for human consumption. They are, in fact, one of the favorite foods for the computers. For more than 20 years years, index funds were the main course for black box traders. Today, a robo trader can influence every single component of the system by trading ETFs. ETFs are much cheaper than index funds and more versatile. They are the fast food for algorithmic traders.

For today's investor, **the most important weapon in their arsenal is the inverse or short ETF.** Investopedia defines an inverse ETF as " an exchange-traded fund (ETF) that is constructed by using various derivatives for the purpose of profiting from a decline of an underlying benchmark. Investing in these ETFs is similar to holding various short positions, or using a combination of advanced investment strategies to profit from falling prices. Also known as a short ETF or bear ETF." (57 words) In other words, when prices go down, inverse ETFs go up. (11 words) If the long position goes down by 3%, the inverse ETF goes up 3%. Leverage can increase the rewards of short ETFs as well as magnify their risk.

There are some incredible advantages for short ETFs: you don't need a margin account, losses are limited to your purchase price, they trade like stocks, are highly liquid, and are approved for IRA accounts. I don't want to confuse anyone, but the beauty is, you can buy the short side by being long. You can buy low and sell high. This seems to be more compatible with investor psychology than a short sale where you buy high and sell low.

How lucrative can the inverse (short) ETF be? In four weeks, DUST jumped 110% in value as volume increased by a factor of 10X! Who were the beneficiaries of this monster move? It was almost exclusively the black box traders. So far, I can't find a single human who ever heard of DUST. Inverse ETFs are almost always short term trades rather than long term investments. To be a happy camper, never ever buy a short ETF on anything making new 52 week highs. New 52 week lows are the proper domicile for inverse ETFs.

The real question for you becomes who do you want to accept investment data from to make buy and sell decisions? For me, the computers are the winners by a huge margin. The computers don't smoke, drink, use dope, get angry, get depressed, lie or cheat their customers. Computers don't work on commissions. I love the computers because in the right situations, they are highly predictable. They buy when they should and sell when they are supposed to.

You live under the mode of an antique investment thinking that makes you a one trick pony. The financial advice you get comes from a 1934 view of the stock market based on Graham and Dodd's <u>Modern Securities Analysis</u>. I challenge any one to go back and take a look at 1934 and then tell me how they are related to today's markets? While you are at it, tell me how a 1934 telephone is similar to today's smart phones or how a 1934 Ford Tri-motor airplane compares to a modern jet? I looked at 1934's stock market very closely,you can find a micro film copy of the WSJ in any public library. Here's what I found. A stock market that covered one page. There were zero listed derivatives of any kind, the Dow 30 wasn't an investment, there wasn't any S&P 100, S&P500, NASDAQ 100 or Russell 2000. It was a plain vanilla and very small stock market. By the way, everything was done by human hands.

Only Wall Street would ignore the realities of a modern, 21st century, computer driven stock market. They control 100% of the media, so for them it's still a world of P/E's and capitalization's. Ask your broker about computerized trading and all you'll get is a blank stare. I challenge you to name any other industry today that ignores the impact of computers like Wall Street? Wall Street is so far behind the curve, they are stuck in a 20th century mode of thinking in a 21st century world. They live in a dream world that is a fantasy land.

Finally, this is a book of numbers. If you can't appreciate numbers, this book, may not be your cup of iced tea. But you should never forget, numbers are the ONLY thing computers feed on when trading. For computers, numbers are, their trump card, and the most important piece in a chess game.

If good science is based on time and a large sample size, this project is quality science. The data goes back 25 years, a quarter of a century (1987-today). The sample size was more than a one hundred and fifty thousand numbers. For 1,300 (and counting) consecutive week ends, I have collected the data this book is based on. If you do anything 1,300 times, you get pretty good at it. The computers can tell you what to buy and when to sell with amazing accuracy, but they can't tell you how much to risk. Only your brain can answer the question, big bet, small bet, or no bet at all?

It's your money, only you can cast off the shackles of 1934 Wall Street thinking or you can embrace the benefits of using computer based behavior to make your investment decisions. The choice belongs to you!

Why the Gold System?

I had a half a dozen systems that I could have written a book about. There was the Major Market Index, Dow 30, S&P 100, S&P 500, NASDAQ 100, the oil sector or gold. The Major Market Index was too small and a minor league player in computerized trading. The S&P 100, S&P 500 and NASDAQ 100 were too large. The Dow 30 was a very close second and I sometimes wonder if it should have been number one? The oil sector has always been a favorite of mine going all the way back to the 1970's. In structure it is similar to gold with a division between explorers (miners) and refiners. The oil sector was both large and complex. Oil came in a close third place. The silver system was so small that it didn't win, place or show.

The gold system was just right, not too large or complex to be understood. It had all of the components of the larger systems in bite size chunks. If you could learn the mechanics of gold then you could master all of the larger systems. Learn about the gold system and subdue all the equities: the Dow 30, S&P 500, the NASDAQ 100, and the Russell 2000. Learn about the gold system and you can rule over all the commodities. Learn about the gold system and you can dominate the world's currencies. Learn about the gold system and you will be the monarch over bond land. If you were to learn about the gold system, you will be the regent in all markets, bull or bear.

The second reason for gold is it has ALWAYS been a hot button issue. Gold is an emotion not just an investment. Yell "Microsoft" in a crowd and a few might react. Yell "GOLD" in a crowd and people are going to pay attention. Gold is, was, and will always be a barometer of our feelings.

The stage is set. The actors are on their marks. The house lights dim and the curtain slowly goes up. Behold, center stage is our star attraction, GOLD.

Our Love Affair With Gold

We have been in love with gold for more than 5,000 years. Gold is very rare, ranking 58th in scarcity. While hard to find, gold can be found on every continent. Gold is very soft and exceptionally malleable. An ancient artisan could pound out one ounce (28 grams) to cover 300 square feet. It is extremely ductile and a single ounce can be spun into a wire 50 miles long or the distance between Long Beach to Laguna Beach in Southern California. Our passion for gold is intense because it seems so indestructible. Gold does rust in air or water.

After 126 years of being exposed to the brutal Atlantic Ocean, gold coins recovered from the wreck of the S.S. Central America were in pristine condition.

Every rose has a thorn and gold is no different. For gold, the thorn is its weight. Gold has a very high molecular density. Gold has a specific gravity of 19.6 or it takes 19.6 ounces of water to displace a single ounce of gold. A tennis ball size of gold would weigh a stunning 5.7 pounds! As the world of commerce grew larger and more complex the use of gold as money became very problematic. To solve the problem the universe of physical gold morphed into the realm of paper money. About 1000 AD, the Song Dynasty in China first issued paper money with disastrous results. The paper money experiment failed as rampart inflation and a bloody civil war ended the rule of the Songs.

We trust gold more than we trust paper. In times of uncertainty and danger we turn to gold. We always have and we always will. Whether it's puppy love or obscene lust, humans love gold.

The Modern Gold Trading System

The modern gold trading system is an electronic spider web of interconnected computers. The most recent system is at least a fourth generation entity and is by far, the most complex. It is in a constant state of change with new parts being added all the time. The system is very fragmented, falls under the rules and regulations of many different authorities, but there is no one in charge of the over all system. Any one can add a new part without any regard on how it will effect other parts of the system. This makes for a volatile and dangerous trading platform.

In the Beginning

The first gold trading market lasted for over 100 years. In the beginning, gold trades were done in something called the "pit" where gold was bought and sold by public outcry. It was a mano a mano spectacle where combatant's weapons were a loud voice and nerves of steel. The trades were recorded on scraps of paper and turned over for reconciliation to clerks who worked under conditions like something straight out of a Dicken's novel. Prices for all gold investments were based on the spot or cash price of gold. The pulse of this gold trading market was the psychology of greed and fear and not a stream of electricity. By the 1860's, electricity was used to transmit gold prices over dedicated telegraph lines to traders from coast to coast.

The historical low light of the first gold trading market was the first Black Friday, September 24, 1869 when Gould and Fisk cornered the gold market. As Directors of the Erie Railway, Jay Gould and Jim Fisk were the original poster boys for bad behavior on Wall Street. They used the Erie as their personal piggy banks and watered Erie stock to the detriment of its shareholders. Gould and Fisk operated during the no rules, anything goes hey day of the stock market.

In 1896, Gould and Fisk hatched a plan to corner the gold market in New York City. Gold was trading in the doldrums in a very narrow range of $125 to $130 an ounce. For the corner to work, Gould and Fisk hatched a conspiracy of magnificent and mammoth complexity. The plot would involve the brother in law of the President, Abel Corbin, the President of the United States, US Grant, high ranking Army officers, Boss Tweed, corrupt big man of Tammany Hall, a corrupt bank, the Tenth National bank to write $20 million in hot checks, corrupt politicians in Albany, New York and a corrupt Federal Judge who was bought off for a million bucks in cash!

By manipulating the press and using President Grant, Gould and Fisk were able to manipulate the price of gold up to $140 an ounce. They held the supply of gold as their hostage and controlled nearly the entire supply of gold in NYC. Bears couldn't sell without buying from them and Bulls couldn't buy anywhere else except from Gould and Fisk. They had the NY gold market by the short hairs and were ready to spring the trap on gold traders on Friday, September 24th, 1869.

As the market opened, Fisk was pushing the price of gold higher by buying and Gould was selling to lock in profits. Higher and higher the price of gold flew. At $163 an ounce, all hell broke out as the price was broken by news the Feds were selling gold in huge quantities. Of course, Gould and Fisk had been warned in advance. On Friday, it was estimated that a stunning $500 million of gold changed hands. Clearly, speculators were selling gold they did not own to gamblers who didn't have the money to pay for it! How did Gould and Fisk make out? I think they made more than anyone at the time ever dreamed. It is just my feelings, but I think Gould sold his long position at $150 an ounce and shorted gold at the same price. When gold closed at near $133 and ounce, they made a huge bundle of dough.

The causes of the Panic of 1869 were unregulated derivatives, excessive leverage, corrupt banks, and greedy politicians. Not all that different from the Market Crash of 2008. In both cases, no one would go to jail. To close, I would like to clear up a historical slur. Jay Gould was not a money grubbing Jew. He was a money grubbing Christian.

The Second Gold Trading Market

The second gold trading market was born in 1975 and lasted a mere ten years. In 1975, trading in gold for future delivery begins on New York's Commodity Exchange and on Chicago's International Monetary Market and Board of Trade. Gold trading broke into two different camps: industrial users and speculators. Industrial users were focused on gold spot prices and speculators lived and died by the values of futures contracts. The actual entry of buy and sell orders were pretty much the same as the old system, the public out cry and use of hand signals, but big changes were in the wind

In 1971, President Richard Nixon was being crushed between a rock and a hard place. The rock was runaway inflation, a ballooning national debt, and an increasing trade imbalance. The hard place was a falling US dollar and the 1944 Bretton Woods Agreement. Under Bretton Woods, the dollar was fixed at $35 an ounce and borrowers could redeem debt in either dollars or gold. By 1971, gold coverage (gold reserves) had been cut by more than fifty percent. The US was printing too many dollars and gold reserves were dwindling. First, the Swiss demanded $50 million in gold followed by France's request for nearly $200 million in gold. The crap really hit the fan when the Great Britain put the squeeze on the US for $ 3 billion dollars of gold from Fort Knox! This was nearly a total of 30% of all US gold reserves and provoked President Nixon to take a radical approach to the issues that were confronting him.

On August15, 1971, President Nixon shocked the world when he imposed a 90 day freeze on wages and prices, slapped a 10% surtax on all imports and closed the gold window. In a single night, without Congressional debate or approval, Tricky Dick had swindled the entire world in what must be history's biggest gold heist. The gold window would reopen with some Mickey Mouse floating rates, but by 1973, the window was closed for good. Foreign countries that had initially borrowed US dollars backed by gold were repaid with dollars backed by fiat. Bretton Woods was nothing more than a memory and a history lesson.

Change was in the air and 1973 would be a stunner. In 1933, FDR signed Executive Order 6102 that forbid Americans from owning gold coins, gold bullion, or gold certificates. The reasoning was gold hoarding was causing the

Great Depression. For me, that's like blaming brain cancer on acne. Four decades later, President Gerald Ford signed Public Law 93-373 that again allowed Americans to own gold. Less than 2 years later, Americans could speculate in gold all they wanted with the trading of gold futures. The grand casino for betting on gold was open for business.

The Third Wave

The third trading market mirrored the changes in the the tone, tenor and conduct of the bigger stock markets. The beginnings of a new world market order started earlier with the advent of Instinet and were accelerated with the new Designated Order Turnaround (DOT) where orders were bundled electronically rather than being routed to the floor of the NYSE. About this time, the new Third Market was being introduced where NYSE stocks could be traded on the OTC. By 1982 with the introduction of S&P 500 futures, the markets were moving towards full automation. No humans need apply. I miss Paul Kangas of the Nightly Business Report who almost every day blamed massive moves in the markets to "computer cowboys." And he was right. Computerized program trading was the rage of the day. Today, we have given it the high and mighty name of algorithmic trading but its real name is "market manipulation."

Out of sheer curiosity, on April 24th, 1998, I mentally painted my first schematic drawing of the gold market using the Wall Street Journal(WSJ). It was a rough outline of the trading route that gold traveled to its many different parts. While the WSJ is a first rate source of business 4-1-1, it is strictly third rate for the food of stock pickers, data. It would be almost useless, except for one tiny, itsy bitsy section that was worth its weight in gold and justifies it's current two buck price.

The Modern Gold Trading Market

The fourth generation, the world in which we live in today,started out with failure and rejection. In early 2002, an Exchange Traded Fund (ETF) backed by gold proposed by India was turned two big thumbs down. I wonder if it was because the India gold market is really run like a massive pawn shop or racial prejudice? The modern gold trading market was born on March 2003, half way around the world in Australia. The world's first gold backed ETF was listed on the Australian Stock Exchange under Gold Bullion Securities under the symbol "GOLD." Gold Bullion Securities were fully backed by the deposit of physical gold which were also fully insured. The idea was to give investor's the ability to own gold and gain exposure to gold price movements without the hassle of storing physical gold bars. It was a brilliant idea and it wouldn't be long before the concept began to move West. In short order, ETF's will become the leading growth portion of the modern gold trading system.

For American investors, the new world order of electronic gold investments started with the opening bell on Thursday, November 18th, 2004 with the introduction of an ETF that specifically tracked gold price movements directly. Sponsored by the World Gold Council under the ticker symbol GLD, the fund was designed to reflect the performance of gold bullion with each share representing the value of one tenth of an ounce of gold. By 2011, investors could cull through a list of 20 different gold backed ETF's. They range from a plain vanilla flavor like GLD and IAU to super complex mixture like the Factor Shares 2X Gold Bull/ S&P 500 Bear (FSG). Today, an investors in Emporia Kansas can mimic the sophisticated trading strategies of a hedge fund with the click of a mouse. Is this what we really want, to be able to mimic a hedge fund?

I have always been blessed with the ability to take three giant steps backwards and be able to see the "big picture" or the forest through the trees. I don't think any one was looking for the gold trading system and given how the data is presented, it would be pretty tough to imagine or " see ." We live in a world of compartments and subdivisions and financial newspapers like the WSJ, Investor's Business Daily (IBD) and Barron's are no different. It doesn't matter which one is your favorite, they all present data about gold in different sections on different pages so you don't get the sense they are all connected.

On Thursday, November 19th 2009, I bought copies of the WSJ and IBD, took them home and separated them page by page on the living room floor. It looked like I was trying to house train a giant Saint Bernard dog! I carefully went through each paper looking for any investment with the names "gold" or "silver." It was like a massive puzzle. For example,.with IBD, I found the heading of "Mutual Funds" and there were listings for funds like "Gbl Gold Eq." and under the heading of NYSE there was Barrick Gold (ABX). I didn't abstract any particular investments but only clipped the headings at this point. After scanning both papers I ended up with a dozen headings which I taped to a single sheet of paper. To verify the parts, I matched the headings with Barron's on the week end. Once you had all the pieces together on one single sheet of paper, you could "see" how all the different parts worked together as a unit or system. I used the same technique to construct trading universes for the S&P500, S&P100, Nasdaq 100, Major Market Index, the Dow 30, and the oil trading systems. It was strictly a labor of love and I can't even begin to tell you what I saw. I glanced at the Russell 2000, but it held absolutely zero interest for me. The modern gold trading system looked like this:

The Components of the Modern Gold Trading System

Cash/Spot Prices	Commodities Futures	Stocks
	Gold (CMX) 100 troy oz.	NYSE
	Gold (CBOT) 33.3 troy ounce	NASDAQ
	Silver (CMX) 5,000 troy ounce	NYSE Market
	Silver (CBOT) 1,000 troy ounce	NYSE Arca

Stock Index	Mutual Funds	Closed End Funds
PHLX Gold/Silver Index		
Amex BUGS Index		
ETF's	Options;	
Bullion	CBOE	
Gold Mining Stocks	Philadelphia	
Long	Nasdaq	
Short	ISEC	

Rather than one big system like the S&P 500, there were really four different systems. One for gold and another for silver. Each of those systems further fragmented into two mutually exclusive systems: one for the miners and another for bullion.

I didn't list the different parts in a straight line or column because the different components look more like a circuit as the parts are all located in different geographical parts of the country. While I used three different sources to construct the system, you can ONLY follow or "read" it by using the 52 Week Highs and 52 Week Lows section of the WSJ! I've been intimate with every part of the system, but if you are new to the game, you might need a score card to clarify them.

Gold Bullion

The cash price is also called the spot price. These prices reflect the buying and selling of a variety of actual or physical commodities in the marketplace separate from the futures price. It is the "now" price of gold. The cash price is what you would pay or receive if you bought physical gold today. It is very important if you are selling a gold candle stick or gold coins. If you don't know the spot price, how do you know if you are getting a good deal or being swindled? The cash price isn't reflected in the day to day valuations of the different parts of the electronic trading system like mutual funds, index funds, ETFs or stocks. Who fixes the price of gold bullion? That answer can be found 94 years ago on September 12, 1919. In the first part of the 20th century, London was the center of the gold refining and bullion sales for the entire world. In 1919, a consortium of banks set the initial fixing price of gold at $20.67 a troy ounce.

Today, London is still the epicenter of the gold bullion price fixing cosmos. Twice a day, 10:30AM and 3:00PM, a consortium of five banks set the world wide spot price for gold. Given the five hour time difference between London and New York City, it's 5:30AM in the Big Apple and most brokers are still asleep with visions of hookers dancing in their heads. Out in LA, it's 2:30 AM and a lot of brokers are getting the last call for alcohol at their favorite bar or strip club.

Today, a conference call between five banks set the price of gold. It's called the London fixing. Those five banks are: Barclays Capital, Deutsche Bank, HSBC Bank, Societe Generale, and the Bank of Nova Scotia The process seems relatively straight forward. There is an opening price which is relayed to the bank's traders and customers. The bankers then declare whether they are buyers or sellers at that price. The lead bank adjust the price until the buyers and sellers are in harmony. On a good day, the process takes less than five minutes. On a volatile day, it might takes fifteen minutes to balance the buyers and sellers.

The importance of the spot price can not be underestimated. Refiners use it to settle contracts, central banks as a bench mark, and it is important to refiners as well as investors.

In 2013, the CFTC began a probe to see if there was any manipulation of spot prices by the five banks. There was a just cause for the investigation. All five banks,as well as eleven other international banks, were targeted for investigation in the massive Libor scandal. The 2012 investigation into the gigantic, world wide London Interbank Offering Rate scandal, would expose a gargantuan conspiracy to fix Libor. The biggest offender? Barclay's Bank, who would pay massive world wide fines without admitting to any guilt. I do believe that Deutsche Bank (DB) was found innocent.

Up to this point, there has been no resolution to the 2013 CFTC gold price fixing inquiry. Mums the word. "No Comment" from anyone involved. Dead silence. Makes you wonder? Let me be clear, I don't have an ax to grind with anyone in this inquiry. But I do think the CFTC is going down the wrong road here and asking the wrong questions. It's like asking someone suffering from cancer whether they are dying from a cold? The CFTC should not be asking questions about price collusion but real tough questions about conflicts of interest! How is it possible that DB sets the price of gold and silver while operating the world's largest (and most aggressive) bullion ETFs without a massive conflict of interest? I am not holding my breath waiting for any answers.

The fixing of silver bullion takes place in the same place, London, at a different time with a smaller consortium of banks. The silver price fixing happens at noon. The three banks involved are: the Bank of Nova Scotia, DB, and HSBC. They use the same bidding process as gold to fix the price of silver.

The Gold Futures

The number one, single most important part of the modern gold trading system is the futures contract. Just like the Sun, the futures are the center of the universe and all other gold investments orbit around it. Every other part of the system is **directly** or **indirectly** valued by its price. It doesn't matter what you own, gold mining stocks, gold mutual funds, or gold based ETF's, you need to keep one eye on your investments and the other eye of the futures contract. Price changes in the futures contract will tell you how to behave. They will clearly let you know when to hold them (buy) and when to fold them (sell).

Futures and options contracts are kissing cousins. They are both derivatives and have the same general parts: standardized underlying assets, 100 ounces for the futures and 100 shares for the options. Both contracts feature standardized expiration dates and the value of the contracts will change based on the never ending battle between the bulls and bears. It is the sheer genius of the standardized contract that will insure the liquidity of both contracts. No lawyers need apply.

The significant difference and it's a big one is the options contract carries a right to make a choice and the owners of the futures face the obligation of fulfilling of the contract. The owner of the options contract may exercise the terms of the contract or simply can walk away. Futures contract owners on both sides of the deal must fulfill terms of the contract on the settlement date. Finally, both contracts are exchange traded derivatives. The exchange's clearing house acts as a counter party on all contracts guaranteeing both sides of the trades, set the margin requirements and provides the mechanism for settlement.

For precious metals, there are two gold commodity futures contracts and two silver commodity futures contracts. For gold, the larger gold futures contract is for 100 troy ounces and traded on the Comex (CMX), to calculate the daily value of the contract, simply multiply the settlement price times 100. For example, if the settlement price was $1475 an ounce, the contract is worth 100 X $1,475 or $147,500. The mini gold futures contract is for 33.2 troy ounces and traded on the Chicago Board of Trade (CBOT). To calculate the value of the mini gold futures contract, you simply multiply the settlement price times 33.2. For example, if the settlement price was $1,475 an ounce, the contract is worth 33.2 X $1475 or $48,970. The mini contract affords its bettors an immense level of leverage. These contracts are not exact mirrors of each other. They have different settlement dates, trade on different exchanges, posses different margin rates and claim different settlement prices. If you think the lure of the leverage of the mini gold futures contract would make them more popular than the bigger contract, you'd be wrong. The larger contracts are favored by traders with a ten to one advantage over the mini's. IBD shows both contracts while the WSJ sticks with the old grandad on the Comex(CMX). Later the mini's would migrate to the CMX via merger, a last minute event after this was written.

There are two silver commodity futures contracts, just like gold. The larger contract is for 5,000 troy ounces and trades on the Comex(CMX). If the silver's contract settled at $40 an ounce, the contract was worth $200,000. The mini silver futures contract is for 1,000 troy ounces and trades on the Chicago Board of Trade (CBOT). If the silver mini settled at $40 an ounce, the mini would cost you $40,000. The large silver futures contracts swamp the mini's by a whopping 15:1 or better ratio.

While I admire the gold and silver futures contracts as the center for the source of power for a massive system of interconnected computers, I do not, cannot, and will not now or ever recommend them as investments for retail (individual) investors. Unless your last name is Gates or Buffett, the low margin requirements and the limit down, lock you into a losing position, make them more dangerous than an eight foot diamond back rattler. While every serious gold investor should always have a rough map inside their head of the trading range of gold futures, from the low (support) to high (resistance). You should have a keen sense of where the current settlement price fits in the map. When it comes to investing in gold there's lots of ways to skin the cat, but futures isn't one of them for the retail investor.

The Commodities Exchange, Inc., the Comex (CMX) is a principal division of the New York Mercantile Exchange (NYMEX) which is the world's largest physical futures exchange. It's head- quarters is located in Manhattan, NYC with satellites in Boston, Washington DC, Atlanta, Dubai, London, and Tokyo. An electric pulse that originates in NYC speeds around money centers through out the world. If you are addicted to super high speed games, this is the ultimate rush.

I don't believe for a second the people at the Comex are crooks, but there is a very big problem at the exchange. In 2009, holders of Comex gold futures experienced problems taking delivery of their metal. Along with systematic delivery delays, some investors have received delivery of gold bars NOT matching their contract in weight and serial numbers. The delays cannot be dismissed as slow warehouse movements, as daily reports show low activity. There are valid concerns that COMEX may not have the gold inventory to back its current warehouse receipts. In plain English, the CMX may be trading "phantom gold." As a result, authorities are considering placing position limits of the CMX. Any changes at the CMX will ripple through the rest of the system.

Mini gold and silver futures trade on the Chicago Board of Trade (CBOT), the world's oldest futures and options exchanges. On March 17th, 2008, Chicago based CME group engineered a friendly merger with NYMEX Holdings, Inc. After the deal closed in August 2008, the new corporate entity handles exchanges for the New York Mercantile Exchange, COMEX. The Chicago Mercantile Exchange and the Chicago Board of Trade (CBOT). Its one big daddy, the CME, with four kids. The CBOT and its kids would join the CMX shortly after this was written. Constant change is the only 100% predictable part of the modern gold trading system.

The biggest single threat to every part of the system is the continuing drive for ever more and more leverage. Gold futures would be no different. To attract degenerate gamblers, the CME began trading a 10 ounce E-micro gold futures contract. Just about everything about the contract would be on a one-tenth scale to the big daddy, 100 troy ounce contract. One tenth the size, one-tenth the margin and one-tenth the trading fees. A big problem is you cannot take delivery of a ten ounce bar of gold. There is little doubt, the new E-micro contract is designed to catch small, individual investors in its net. According to Joe Raia, CME managing director of energy products and services, the new 10-ounce E-micro would allow investors the chance for more trading flexibility, an efficient way to adjust positions, and a means of attracting retail clients. Don't kid yourself. The ten ounce contract is nothing more than bloody chum in the water for gambling addict sharks.

Today, in the WSJ, you can easily find data on the 100 troy ounce, the 50 troy ounce mini NY contracts in the "Futures Section." I can usually find the numbers blindfolded. The 100oz. Gold big boy, the 50 ounce and the 10 oz are not fit for human consumption. They are the electronic food of computers.

Anytime you have futures contracts there is always the potential for market manipulation and gold futures are a prime example. If you believe in conspiracy theories and market manipulation, then the report by Jason Hamlin is your cup of peach tea. Mr. Hamlin replicates the earlier work of whistle blower, Andrew Maguire. The scam starts at nearly the same time of the trading month with just 2-3 days prior to the expiration dates for gold futures, gold stocks, and options. Just prior to the expiration date, either in futures or options, traders short increase their net short positions in order to drive gold futures and stocks down. This move allows the manipulators, primarily four "anonymous" large investment banks to profit as the contracts they sold to innocent chumps expire worthless. The sudden and steep price decline gives the manipulator's the chance to cover their short positions making a bundle by paying back their creditors with lower priced gold or stocks. While the average manipulated drop in gold averaged between \$12 to \$30, the three day period between May 19th and May 21st, 2010 fueled a massive \$43 drop in gold prices. That is a lot of dough for the pigs at the trough to feast on.

After details of this swindle were very clearly explained to the Commodities Futures Trading Commission (CFTC), nothing was done to stop the obvious manipulation of gold futures Is this a matter of corruption or incompetence by the CFTC? I don't think so, but may mask an even bigger problem for the CFTC. If the CFTC acknowledges gold futures being used to manipulate gold prices, they might open a can of giant night crawlers and have to deal with the gargantuan problem of manipulation of the S&P 500! I was extremely disappointed no one had the stones to identify the four large investment banks at the center of this scam. How can we hold these creeps accountable if we can't call them out by name?

If you believe in market manipulation theories, check your calendar 2-3 days before the expiration of gold futures, gold options, and stock options. These days may provide a buying opportunity when gold prices are manipulated downward?

Gold Mining Stocks

I love common stocks with an uncommon passion. Why the love? It's because common stocks are the most flexible and versatile investments under the Sun. They are only limited by one's imagination. You can use common stocks to make money when prices go up and when they go down. You can own them for a day, week, month or forever. You can fund a lifestyle with their income. Every single component of the gold trading system is based on a unique form of legal ownership and common stocks are no different. There are a lot of benefits to owning common stocks: free transferability, limited liability, and an asset that doesn't fade away with the death of its founder. The corporation cannot dilute your ownership without your permission and in most cases you have the right to vote on important corporate matters. The downside to owning common stocks is in the case of bankruptcy. You are last in line to recover any assets and will probably be wiped out financially. From hero to zero!

For over150 years, the heart of gold trading was the ownership of gold mining stocks. The problem has always been the same: gold mining stocks trend in the direction of gold prices, but do not track it on a dollar for dollar basis. There are days, gold mining stocks will race slightly ahead of gold futures and other days, when their prices will slightly lag. It is a very rare day when gold stocks prices will differ significantly from the gold futures. The difference is measured in nickels and dimes, not big wads of dough. They generally dance in the same direction, but like all partners, they sometimes get out of step. You can find a menu of gold mining stocks in the 1,000 largest section of the WSJ, starting with Anglo Gold Ashanti ADS and ending with Yamana Gold. There are about ten different gold mining stocks in between ranging from big names to little known players on the NYSE in the 1,000 largest list. There are many other gold mining stock players in different parts the NYSE like NYSE Market and NYSE Arca.

My first paramour in gold mining stocks was Homestake Mining (HM). Homestake was the stuff that legends were built on. The first legends in the story of Homestake were Col. George A. Custer and Chief Sitting Bull. They resolved their issues at the Battle of the Little Big Horn. Two years before the battle, Custer had invaded South Dakota in search of gold and farm land. The following rush by gold miners set the stage for the total annihilation of the Seventh Calvary. Soon another legend would cast a giant shadow, George Hearst. Hearst was a hard drinking, nicotine addict who loved to gamble. Hearst played hardball in a slow pitch league. To build Homestake he used every dirty trick in the book including murder. He would father William Randolph Hearst, the "King of Yellow Journalism"and one of the richest men in the world. George Hearst would become a US senator and die in his San Francisco palace in 1891 at the age of 70.

Custer's blood would hardly be dry on the ground before two miners would discover the great Homestake gold and silver deposit. In 1877, George Hearst and two business partners bought the claim for a mere $70,000! Hearst and his partners sold shares of Homestake Mining Company (HM) to the public via a stock offering and it was listed on the NYSE in1879. Its 145 year run made HM one of the longest running shows on the Big Board. HM produced 40 million ounces of gold and 10 tons of silver in its life. Not bad for a $70,000 original investment. The gold ore at Homestake was always poor quality where less than one ounce of gold was produced for every one ton of ore. Homstake would be de-listed in 2002 just as the gold boom was beginning. For the next ten years I would follow Barrick Gold Mines (ABX). In 2010, I would stop following gold mining stocks in favor of gold mining ETFs.

Preferred stock is a special equity security that has the features of both a stock and bond. Generally considered a hybrid, preferreds are senior to common stock at dissolution of a company but are subordinate to corporate bond's. Preferreds come in many different flavors and I had a a brief fling with convertible preferred's. Under the right conditions you could sell calls against the conversion ratio, but it was a hassle finding them .Preferreds are usually bought by conservative investors seeking income, but buyer beware as interest rates go up, their value goes down just like a bond. Anglo Gold Ashanti PrA is an example of this part of the system.

The Exchanges

Of all the changes to the modern gold trading system, the stock exchanges will suffer the most. These changes have turned the once might New York Stock Exchange (NYSE) into a toothless, old, paper tiger. Today, the NYSE accounts for a puny 25% of stock trades or a mere 250 million shares for every one billion shares traded. It has been reduced to a photo op back drop for news reports and a place where big wigs get to ring the opening and closing bell. The new buzz word for trading stocks is "proprietary platforms." and ECN's. Investment firms don't want to conform to the rules of the NYSE which were designed to protect the best interests of investors. These firms want a world of "dark pools." "spoofing," "sniffing," and the ability to paint the tape with millions of bogus trades and the best interests of the public be darned. It's really all about cheating someone out of one thousandths of a single penny. The NYSE is the world's largest exchange is terms of capitalization, but not in the number of shares traded every day.

It is operated by NYSE Euronet which was born by the NYSE's merger with the fully electronic stock exchange Euronet. The original powerhouses of the NYSE, men who owned seats on the exchange were bought out and are nothing but a memory. NYSE Euronet operates and holds stakes in: the NYSE, Euronet, NYSE Arca, and the NYSE Amex. It also owns a bunch of trading plat- forms I've never heard of: NYSE Arca Europe, NYSE Alternet, NYSE Technologies, Inc., Easy Next, Blue Next, Free Market and Smart Pool. As of April 2011, the whole shooting match was on the seller's block with the lead dog bidder being Germany's Bourse. After rejecting a higher bid from rivals NASDAQ and ICE, this dog is headed for the court's. I wonder if this is a case of be careful of what you wish for?

What is the future of the NYSE? Writer Daniel Randall believes it's a good bet the NYSE will become NYC's number one party place after the completion of a new make over. There isn't any amount of make up that can change the reality that the NYSE isn't what she used to be. The conversion of the NYSE from the center of the investment universe to a party glitter dome and photo op made for TV set spells trouble for the world at large. It is the destruction of the NYSE that has turned the investments into a world wide 24 X 7 casino. The future of stock trading has shifted from NYC to places like Lenexa, Kansas, home of BATS. BATS stands for Better Alternative Trading System ™ and is an electronic stock exchange. No humans need apply. Founded in 2005, BATS is the third largest exchange in volume behind the NYSE and NASDAQ.

The American Stock Exchange was always a junior varsity to the varsity team, NYSE. The Amex's initial purpose was to trade in stocks that couldn't meet NYSE listing requirements. They traded outside the NYSE, were known as "curb brokers" and didn't move indoors until late 1921. From 1971 to 2008, the Amex would fight tooth and nail against being merged with the varsity team, the NYSE. The Amex gave up the fight and after the merger, the old Amex Curb Exchange building was closed and trading moved to the floor of the NYSE. After numerous name changes, today its formal moniker is NYSE Amex Equities and as the weakest sister of all the exchanges stands the greatest chance of total extinction. Examples of gold mining stocks on the NYSE Amex system are:Gold Resources (GORO), Great Basin Gold A (GBG), MAG Silver (MVG) and New Gold (NGD). When it comes to gold mining stocks on the NYSE Amex, can you spell s-p-e-c-u-l-a-t-i-v-e?

The NASDAQ is the largest electronic equity trading market in the US and second largest by market capitalization in the world. There are 2,872 listings on NASDAQ and by trading volume is the world's number one electronic stock exchange. NASDAQ was the successor of the over the counter (OTC) system of trading. A stock trade here is negotiated between dealers and the mark up is hidden in the disguise of a net trade. In 35 years, I have never used the services of the NASDAQ and I don't see any reason to change. Here are two examples of gold mining stocks traded on the NASDAQ: Royal Gold (RGLD) and Rand Gold Resources ADS (GOLD). If I were looking for entry to the modern gold trading system, the NASDAQ, is the last place I'd look. Just my opinion.

If the NASDAQ is the last place I'd look for gold market system opportunities, the NYSE Arca wins first place, hands down. NYSE Arca is an abbreviation for the Archipelago Exchange. NYSE Arca is a securities exchange where both options and stocks are traded. The appeal for me is the NYSE Arca accounts for 30-40% of the traded volume for exchange traded funds (ETF's).

It's going to turn serious here, if the blitz of words has made you groggy, I suggest taking a short break. Perhaps building and monitoring a system of a dozen different parts may cost too much time and may be too much to absorb? Where do you even start? Which part is the filet mignon of the system? Do I have watch all twelve different parts every day? The key to the golden prize is to build a simpler four part sub system with two of those parts are on the NYSE Arca and the other two are commodities futures contracts traded on the CMX. You can accomplish any investment goals you could ever imagine by monitoring the following four parts: the Gold Futures Contract traded on the CMX, the Silver Futures Contract traded on the CMX, the NYSE Arca New 52 Week Highs and the NYSE Arca New 52 Week Lows. The data is in the

"Money&Investing" section of the WSJ. Rather than follow the entire system, if you isolate just these four parts, I guarantee you are going to see a very, very interesting picture. I believe the relationship between the futures and NYSE Arca ETF's will build a betting system more powerful and predictable than the past 15 years of data. I can hardly wait for the next decade of numbers.

Index Funds

Whenever you hear the word "index" in the investment universe, think of the words "mimic" and "mirror image." After you see the innards of one, you can see what they are and how they work. The Philadelphia Gold/Silver Index is a model portfolio of sixteen precious mining companies. Its index components are: Barrick Gold Corp@21.98%, Gold Corp.,Inc.@14.92%, Newmont Mining @14.13%, Freeport McMoran Copper and Gold Inc.@12.92%, Kinross Gold Corp.@7.37%, Anglo GoldAshanti ADS@6.55%, Agnico-Eagle Mines, Ltd.@3.98%, Yamana Gold MiningCo.,Ltd.@3.47%, Harmony Gold Mining@3.13%, Rand Gold Resources ADS@2.34%, PanAmericanSilverCorp.@ 1.19%,Royal Gold Corp.@1.09%, Silver Wheaton@1.06%, Cour D'Alene Mines@.77%, and Silver Standard Resources@.56%. It shouldn't surprise anyone that it takes a basket of 15 stocks to complete a program computerized trade.

An index fund buys and sells stocks in a manner that mirrors the composition of the selected index. If Newmont Mining(NEM) goes up, the fund buys and if NEM goes down, the fund sells. The PHLX Gold/Silver Index is really just a computer model with zero human input as when to sell and how much to buy in the index. No humans need apply.

The PHLX Gold/Silver Index was born on January 1976 and had an initial value of 100. The stock symbol for the PHLX Gold/Silver Index is XAU. Options for the PHLX Gold/Silver Index started trading in December of 1983. For decades, the PHLX Index was the standard for reporting gold price movements. The PHLX is the oldest US stock exchange founded in 1790 and is currently owned by the NASDAQ. With the PHLX Gold/Silver Index trading around 235, the institutions use the index to computer trade (arbitrage) against the gold mining stocks in the index. I can't remember any retail investor ever owning the index. Most retail clients play the options, puts and calls, for the index. I don't know if a Cheetah can change its spots, so years ago I stopped using the PHLX to trade options. Every single time I tried trading options on the PHLX, I got burned using "market orders." A market order calls for the next best available price and my trades were always significantly higher than the previous ask price. So you can give the PHLX options exchange a try, but for me, it's burned twice and I'm gun shy.

There is another gold mining stock index that is more of a cousin than a brother. The new family member was born on March 15,1996 and called the Amex Gold BUGS Index. Its stock ticker is HUI. In the beginning, it had three significant differences from its cousin, XAU. HUI was a modified equal dollar weighted index of gold mining stocks. The stocks had a history of short term hedging of less than two years. Finally, the HUI was more in tune with gold bullion prices than XAU. In the decade of 2000 to 2010, HUI would appreciate by a jaw dropping 1,600%! When you see this kind of price trajectory, it is an invitation, for the aggressively conservative investor to buy calls.

The Amex Gold Bugs Index, today more commonly called the HUI Gold Index is a model portfolio of sixteen gold mining stocks. The components of the HUI Gold Index and their weighting are: Goldcorp@16.20%, Barrick Gold@15.37%, Newmont Mining@10.88%, Harmony Gold ADR@5.23% Coeur d'alene Mines@5.11%, Yamana Gold@5%, Anglogold Ashanti ADR@4.88%, Gold Fields Ltd. ADR@4.80%, Randgold Resources ADR@4.71%, Iamgold-corp@4.43%, Eldorado GoldCorp@4.43%, Hecla Mining@4.14%, Comp de Minas Buenaventura ADS@4.08%, New Gold Inc.,@3.90%, Kinross Gold@3.85%, and Agnico Eagle Mines@3.11%.

XAU or HUI? While HUI is slightly more muscular than XAU and more closely mimics gold bullion prices, in the end, I follow XAU. I have been following XAU since the 1970's and like the fact I can find it in the WSJ in a flash. In a way, it's a push, but you need to follow one in order to control your vision of the gold mining sector of the larger gold trading system.

Mutual Funds

If I dislike the NASDAQ, I truly despise open end funds AKA mutual funds. I don't have very much respect for the financial advisers who peddle them. For me they are selfish, possibly greedy, have the investment imagination of a flea and the courage of a yellow bellied sap sucker. Their sales mantra is the hype of "diversification" and "professional management." Its been my experience, they are over diversified with losers canceling out winners and over managed with some funds turning over faster than a pancake flipper at IHOP. The funds are usually a portfolio of stocks and bonds that are sold at Net Asset Value

(NAV) directly from the fund and can only be sold once a day usually after the market's close. Mutual funds come from "Miss Land." They are sold with misleading sales tactics and completely misunderstood by the investor's who buy them. Given the alternative of ETF's, personally I don't think the world would miss them if they just disappeared from the investment universe. They force investor's to accept the the pain of being long and wrong and in 2008 were the leading cause of investor financial pain.

While most of the world sees investments as numbers I perceive them as electric pulses. I always measure all investments against the costs of that pulse. With mutual funds its just not paying a huge amount for the original pulse, it's that you have to repay for it over and over again by the way of very aggressive management fees. Its like I went to my favorite restaurant, the Black Angus, bought my favorite prime rib dinner(medium rare) and then had to pay for the "memory" of that dinner for the rest of my life. Excessive management fees, ranging from 1-3% a year means a giant mutual fund vacuum cleaner is sucking money from you even if the fund is a dog. Over a long period of time, they can make more money than you in a poor performing fund. It just isn't that mutual funds are hyper expensive to buy and maintain, they are tax traps. Before you buy any mutual fund, ask your financial adviser to explain what an "unrealized capital gain" is? Ask them how it's possible for the NAV to go down and for you to owe taxes at the same time?

According to Investor's Business Daily (IBD), there are less than a dozen gold based mutual funds. I couldn't find any in the WSJ. If you notice, I acknowledge the existence of gold mutual funds as a part of the larger gold trading system. I refuse to grant them any credibility by following their price movements. There are no conditions I can think of why an investor should buy a mutual fund when a gold back ETF can do a better job.

Exchange Traded Funds: ETFs

If a stock index fund had sex with an closed end mutual fund, they'd produce a "love child" named an exchange traded fund (ETF). In my lifetime, nothing would radicalize my view of the entire investment universe than the view I saw through the eyes of ETF's. In 2011, I replaced twelve stocks,some with me since 1987. I added five pairs of matched (long v short) ETF's. Good bye old pals. Next year in 2012, I'm looking forward to dropping two more old friends from 1987 to add two more new ETF's. So why the biggest seismic change in more than twenty years? Parts of an ETF can look like a mutual fund but they act and trade like stocks.. For the retail investor's ETF's offer an undivided interest in a pool of stocks, bonds, or commodities that can be bought and sold like stocks. It goes so far beyond that. For the first time in my life, I can view both sides of the markets, long versus short, at the same time. By matching opposite ETF's, I can see the week by week performance of: 20 year+ Treasury bonds (TBT vs UBT), the S&P 500 (UPRO vs SPXU), the DJIA (DDM vs DXD), the NASDAQ 100 (PSQ vs QQQ), the oil market (UCO vs SCO) and for this project, most importantly, the gold market (DGP vs DZZ). I keep an eye on SLV vs ZSL for the silver market, while I only document the SLV. The new 52 week highs versus the new 52 week lows will tell you when to buy and when to sell.

Some of the gold and silver ETF's are designed to track the bullion prices for gold and silver. This is a significant change from the past 200 years. Today, an investor can index or mirror gold and silver price movements which is a huge leg up on the old trending price model of gold mining stocks. I believe the big plus here is that certain gold ETF's will give investor's an improved chance of future price predictability than the old gold mining stock method. We no longer need to factor things like labor costs, energy costs, balance sheets, styles of corporate management, or investor sentiment in prognosticating about future gold investments when using a select universe of ETF's.

In general, there are three types of gold ETF's: those who own physical gold and silver, some that trade derivatives like futures contracts, and others that are made up of gold mining stocks. Compared to mutual funds, they are cheap to buy and even cheaper to own with minimal manage- ment fess of .6-1%. Less management fees means more money in your bank account. They can be traded any time the stock exchanges are open which gives you more flexibility. I love gold ETF's because you can sell or buy options against the underlying asset, a feature completely lacking in mutual funds.

In 2011, my trading universe in gold and silver ETF's looked like: the matched pair of Power- shares DB Gold Double Long (DGP) and PowerShare DB Gold Double Short (DZZ), Market Vectors Gold Mining (GDX) and iShares Silver Trust (SLV). I am completely blind in my right eye so I keep the left eye focused on PrShrUltShort Silver (ZSL). Next year, I plan to add the following matched pair of ETF's: DIREXIONDAILYGOLDMINER'S 3XBULL (NUGT) and DIREXION- DAILYGOLDMINER'S3XBEAR (DUST).

I think gold backed ETF's are the cat's meow because they are cheap to buy, cheap to own, offer investor's the chance to mirror the price of gold and silver, give investor's the opportunity to turbo charge their ETF's with added income by selling calls, and yield the opportunity to participate in bull and bear gold markets previously unknown to human kind.

We know that gold mining shares trade to a discount or a premium against gold bullion. This the law. I think this distance is highly variable. We do have a fresh insight statistically to the "haircut" between gold mining shares and bullion prices. The following data covers the first four months of 2012.

Gold Mining ETF	SPDR Gold Trust (GLD)
Market Vectors Gold Miners (GDX)	.67
Market Vectors Junior Gold Miner (GDJX)	.72
PowerShares Global Gold and Precious Metals Portfolio (PSAU)	.66
Global X Pure Gold Miners Fund (GGGG)	.57
iShares MSCI Global Miners Fund (RING)	.73

I wonder what the data would look like over a decade or longer? There is a very valuable lesson here. If you want to profit from a move in gold bullion prices, buy a gold bullion ETF over a gold mining stock ETF.

Just like the most beautiful girl in the room with a big fat zit on her chin, ETF's do have a blemish. It's a tax defect, gold backed ETF's are considered a sale of the underlying commodity and taxed at 28% capital gains rates as opposed to lower rates for stocks.

Finally, I've been collecting data for gold stocks for more than 20 consecutive years. I believe, by following a certain sub set of gold ETF's, the future betting model for buy and sell signals will definitely exceed a 50/50 bet.

Listed Options

Options, calls and puts, are available for just about every part of the gold trading system with the notable exception of mutual funds. If I adore ETF's, I am passionately in love with inverse gold ETF's because they free us from the tyranny of puts and the unlimited risks of a short sale. Options trade on five different exchanges with the Chicago Board Options Exchange (CBOE) as its lead dog. The CBOE began trading options in 1973 and well may be one of the greatest investment platforms in the universe. If I could have dinner with any three historical figures it would be Jesus Christ, BF Skinner and the person who invented the Options Clearing Corporation (OCC). Options are an important part of a bigger system where all the parts work in concert with one another. When gold prices are up, the calls increase in value throughout the system and the puts go down. When gold prices are down, the puts increase in value in the system and the calls are lower.

There were three investments who were the subject of the Investment Company Act of 1940. They were open end mutual funds, unit investment trusts (UIT) and closed end funds. It may shock you but there has always been a soft spot in my heart for closed end funds. As a value investor, I always had my eye out for a closed end fund trading at a discount to its NAV. A closed end fund looks like and trades like a stock. It issues a fixed number of shares and is probably the smallest part of the gold system. I could only find daily info on closed end funds in IBD. The two that caught my eye were the Central Gold Trust (GTU) and the Gabelli Global Gold, Natural Resources & Income Trust (GGN). My old pal, Ron Ray from Oklahoma, loved Mario Gabelli and I always listened to what Ron had to say.

Now it is time to look at the modern gold trading system by a series of actual case histories from the WSJ. It was a blast to follow the system and you can do it for yourself using the "Money& Investing" section of the WSJ. You can always find the gold and silver futures on the second to last or last page of the section. The PHLX Gold/Silver Index is a couple of pages from the front of the section and all the rest of the data is buried somewhere else in the paper.

Case History # 1:A Series of New 52 Week Highs

October 5th,2010

Gold and silver have been on a tear since the beginning of the year. The gold futures contract (CMX 100 troy oz.) is up $23.50 to close at $1,338.90, a new high for the year. The silver contract (CMX 5000 troy oz.) closes at $22.51.

A Universe of New 52 Week Highs

The PHLX Gold/Silver Index closes up at 202.88, a new 52 week high. The NYSE yields five new highs. They were: Anglo Gold Ashanti ADS Pfd A (AU-PrA 54.31), ASA (31.79), Freeport Mc Moran (FCX 91.80), Gold Fields ADS (GFI 15.99), and Silver Wheaton (SLW 27.29). The NYSE Amex chimes in with two new winners. They were: Gold Resources (GORO 23.63) and New Gold

(NGD 7.08). The NASDAQ has two new highs. They were: Pwr Shs Gold Prec Metals (PSAU 47.01) and Rangold Resources (GOLD 106.44).

The mother lode of new 52 week highs was found on the NYSE Arca with a dozen gold nuggets. They were all long ETFs: ETFS Gold Tr (SGOL 133.65), ETFS Silver Tr (SIVR 22.82), iShsGold (IAU 19.24), Glbl X Silver Miners (SIL 19.24), iShs Sil Tr (SLV 22.41), PwrShs DB Dbl Gold Long (DGP 38.50), Pwr Shs DB Gold (DGL 47.54), Power Shs Prec Metals (DBP 46.55), Pwr Shs DB Silver (DBS 40.49), Pwr Shs Ultra Gold (UGL 64.05), Pro Shs Ultra Silver (AGQ 92.00) and SPDR Gold Tr (GLD 131.12).

Summary

This is a fascinating picture to see. I wonder what is next on the agenda? It clearly appears that the ignition point in the system was the futures. We shall test that in the future. There were 21 new 52 week highs in the system. Houston, we have blast off!

Case History#2: A Series of Higher Highs

October 14th, 2010

Nine days after the first recorded event in the system, the universe seems on fire with a series of higher highs.

The Universe of New 52 Week Highs

The futures are flying high. The gold futures soar up by $23. 80 to close at $1,369.50. The silver contracts zoom up by 79 cents to close at $23.91.

The PHLX Gold/Silver Index maintains its place in the formation and closes at a record 209.64. The NYSE chimes in with six winners. They were: ASA (32.75), Anglo Ashanti Gold ADS (AU 48.16), Anglo Ashanti Gold Pr A ADS (AU Pr A 55.01), Barrick Gold (ABX 49.66), Freeport Mc Moran (FCX 99.92), and Silver Wheaton (SLW 27.71). The NYSE Amex chips in with four winners.

They were: Gold Resources (GORO 24.27), Great Basin Gold (GBC 2.94), MAG Silver (MVG 8.21) and New Gold (NGD 7.49). The NASDAQ has one winner, Pwr Shs Gold Precious Metals (PSAU 48.68).

The largest squadron of winners was the NYSE Arca with thirteen high fliers. Higher high ETFs were: ETRACS Silver (USV 35.77), ETFS Gold Tr (SGOL 136.80), ETFS Silver Tr (SIVR 23.98), Glbl X Sil Miners (SIL 20.17), iShs Gold Tr (IAU 13.45), iShs Silver Tr (SLV 23.50), Market Vector Gold (GDX 58.82), Junior Mkt Vec Gold (JGDX 36.53), Pwr Shs DB Dbl Gold Long (DGP40.33), Pwr Shs DB Gold (DGL 48.18), Pwr Shs DB Prec Mtls (DBP 47.87) , Pro

ShsDB Silver (DBS 42.45), Pwr Shs Ultra Gold (UGL 67.10), Pwr Shs Ult Sil (AGQ 100.47) and the SPDR Gold Trust (GLD).

The Universe of New 52 Week Lows

The following inverse gold and silver ETFs are making new 52 week lows. This is to be expected. As the prices of gold and silver go, the inverse ETFs will decrease in value. The crash and burn victims in this sub system were: Pwr Shs DB Gold Short ETN (DZZ 8.53), Pwr Sh DBDblGold Short ETN (DGZ 15.67) and ProShs Ultra Short Silver (ZSL 18.46).

Summary

The system is running hot and true. It is in perfect harmony,an universe of symmetry and a world of perfect congruence. There were 23 long winners and three short losers.

Case History#3: Red Scare in Red China

Oct.,19th,2010

It was a day of negatives across the board as Red China hiked interest rates to combat inflation. The rest of the world is fighting the specter of deflation. Also, for market conspiracy buffs we are in the zone where gold futures contracts expire and are subject to price manipulation by a small cabal of investment firms.

The gold and silver futures are negative with gold prices down $36.10 and silver futures plummeting by 63 cents a contract. Oil is off $3.57 a barrel. The Dow is down -165.07, the S&P 500 off -18.11 (a pretty good pop), and the NASDAQ falls -43.71.

There is no ignition point and there are ZERO new 52 week highs to be found anywhere in the entire universe. Zip for the NYSE, nada for the NYSE Amex, ziltch for the NASDAQ and none in the NYSE Arca complex.

Summary

In a way, this is the most valuable intelligence report so far. The system is a complete blank with the only gains in the inverse ETFs. Today, owners of calls are very sad.

Case History# 4: Gold Closes Above $1,400

November 8th, 2010

The Universe of New 52 Week Highs

The futures reignite and the system explodes in an orgy of new 52 week highs. The gold futures close at $1,402.80 and silver futures are up to $27.42. They pull the PHLX Gold/Silver Index to a new 52 week high of 220.61.

The action on the NYSE is red hot with ten mining stocks trading to new highs. The list includes: AngloAshanti Gold ADS (AU 56.77), Anglo Ashanti Gold Pfd A (AuprA 49.94), Barrick Gold (ABX 51.27), Gold Corp (GG 47.88), Gold Fields ADS (GFI 17.28), Hecla Mine (HL 9), Hecla Mine Pfd C (HL pr C 90.48), Silver Wheaton (SLW 35.12), Silver Corp Metals (SVM 12.80), and US Gold Corp (UXG 6.42). The NYSE Amex has six new winners in the new high lotto. They were: Central Gold Tr (GTU 53.49), Fronteer Gold (FRG 9.55), MAG Silver (MVG 10.18), and Nova Gold Res (NGD 14.73). The NASDAQ chimes in with three new highs: Pan Am Silver (PAAS 36.64), Pwr Shs Glb Gold Prec Metals (PSAU 50.99) and Silver Standard (SSRI 26.65).

The Paul Bunyan of the universe continues to be the NYSE Arca sub system. NYSE Arca gives us fourteen new 52 week highs. They were: ETRACS Silver (USV 40.87), ETFS Silver (SIVR 27.65), ETFS Gold Tr (SGOL 140.40), iPath UBS Pr Mtls (JJP 78.62), iShs Sil Tr (SLV 27.15), Mkt Vec Gold(GDX 61.85), Mkt Vec Junior Gold (JGDX 41.99), PwrShs DB Dbl Gold Long (DGP 42.46), Pwr Shs DB Gold (DGL 49.48), Pwr Shs DB Prec Metals (DBP 50.50), Pro Shs Ultra Gold (DGL 70.36) Pro Shs Ultra Silver (AQG 132.37), Sprott Physical Silver (PSLV 11.23, and the SPDR Gold Trust (GLD).

The Universe of New 52 Week Lows

It is the cast of usual inverse ETF suspects. It is lower lows for DZZ 8.09, DGZ 15.21 and ZSL at 13.

Summary

The longs are fat and getting fatter. The universe has grown to 33 winners on the long side. The inverse ETFs are skinny and shrinking in value. El cheapo third tier gold investments are joining the party. Brokers know that cheap stocks in a hot market are easy pickings for gullible buyers.

Case History#5: A Day of Negatives

Tues.,November 16th,2010

The trading day is negative for all sectors of the modern gold trading system with the exception of the inverse ETF sub system. The only truth is I know for sure from the Old School is that markets will fluctuate. Nothing goes up every day and losses are a part of the game.

The gold and silver futures are down as gold falls $30.10 and silver slips by 86 cents. There is no ignition point in the system today. The PHLX Gold/Silver Index plummets by -6.11. Oil dumps $2.52 a barrel. The Dow is down -178.47. The S&P 500 and the NASDAQ are calling in sick today as well. There are zero new 52 week highs and zero new 52 week lows in the system today. Every NYSE gold and silver mining stocks are showing losses for the day.

Is this the beginning of the end or is the market just seeking a level of support? Is it time to run and hide or is this a chance to buy at the low end of the trading range? It is time to buy!

Case History# 6: A Hedge Against Chaos

April 5th,2011

Gold and silver have been trading side ways since late November, 2010. On April 5th, 2011, gold and silver reignite as the world begins to shiver over Europe's sovereign debt crisis.

The Universe of New 52 Week Highs

Gold and silver futures are trading to new highs with gold up to $1,451.80 and silver coming along for the ride going higher to $39.17. While the PHLX Gold/Silver Index is up 9.39, it fails to make a new 52 week high.

The NYSE gives us just three new highs: Cour D Mines (CDE 36.99), Gold Corp (GG 52.18), and Silver Corp Metals (SVM 15.22). NYSE Amex pitches in with one new high: Allied NV Gold (ANV 40.50). The NASDAQ yields no new highs.

NYSE Arca gives us a baker's dozen of thirteen new highs. They were: DBIQ Opt Yld Gold (DGL 51.27), DBIQ Opt Yld Silver (DBG 69.02), ETFS Gold Tr (SGOL 144.82), ETFS Silver Tr (SIVR 39.02), ETFS Asian Gold (AGOL 144.78), Glb Pure Gld Mnrs (GGGG 16.42), Gbl X Silver Mnrs (SIL 30.08), iShs Gold Tr (IAU 14.24), Pwr Shs DB Gold Long (DGP 44.42), Pro Shs Ultra Gold (UGL 73.32), Pro Shs Ultra Sil (AGQ 243.98). RBS Trendpilot (TBAR 26.33) and the SPDR Gold Tr (GLD 142.09).

A Universe of New 52 Week Lows

I know it is a broken record, but the players are all the same: DZZ-7.46, DGZ-14.68 and ZSL-21.31. Summary

While gold shines, the gold miming stocks do not fly as high or shine as brightly. The PHLX Gold/ Silver Index is up, but doesn't reach the stratosphere of new highs. Ten gold mining stocks notch winning numbers for the day but don't make the new high cut. Ignition in the futures only fuels new highs in the long bullion ETF sub system. While gold is up, the universe of winners is only half as big as its former high of 33.

Case History# 7: Gold is Flying High

April 6th,2011

It is a magic week for gold and silver. Unfortunately it doesn't carry over to the PHLX Gold/ Silver Index. As the futures trade higher, the Index goes the other way. Houston, we have a disconnect between the gold bullion rocket ship and the booster of gold mining stocks. It's a small loss, but a break just the same.

The Universe of New 52 Week Highs

Gold futures close up at $1,457 and silver is pushing the $40 an ounce barrier and closes at $39.38. The NYSE yields seven new 52 week highs. They were: Endeavour Silver (EXK 11.85). First Majestic Silver (AG 26.88), Gold Corp (GG 53.86), Harmony Gold ADS (HMY 15.62), Silver Wheaton (SLW 46.94), US Gold Corp (UXG 9.75) and Yamana Gold (AUY 13.21). The NYSE Amex chips in with four new high winners. They were: Capital Gold (CGC 6.45), Extoree Gold (XG 6.95), Fronteer Gold (FRG 15.36, and MAG Silver (MVG 14.78). The NASDAQ gives us one new high winner: Silver Standard (SSRI 34.61).

The NYSE Arca complex contributes thirteen long ETFs to the new 52 week high universe. Many of them are our old favorites riding the crest of a gold price wave. The winners were: DBIQ Opt Yld Gold (DGL 51.46), DBIQ Opt Yld Silver (DBS 69.88), ETFS Gold Tr (SGOL 145.36), ETFS Silver Tr (SIVR 39.57), Glb X Pure Gold Mnrs (GGGG 16.86), Glb X Silver Tr (SIL 130.69), iShs Gold Tr (IAU 14.29), I Shs Sil Tr (SLV 38.82), Pwr Shs DB Gold 2X Long (DGP 44.74), Pwr Shs Ultra Gold (UGL 73.90), Pwr Shs Ultra Sil (AGQ 249.99) Gold Trendpilot (TBAR 26.50) and the SPDR Gold Tr (GLD 142.62).

The New Universe of New 52 Week Lows

Ladies and gentlemen, we have a new player in the world of inverse ETFs. It is new to the system, DXDNDLYGLDMNR2XBEAR (DUST 35.20). I suspect this is not the last we will hear from DUST. Our three old stand byes are in the low lights: DZZ-7.40, DGZ-14.62 and ZSL-20.77.

Summary

There is a small discount in the modern gold trading system as gold mining stocks are lagging behind the new stratospheric highs of the futures. The universe has swollen to twenty five new highs.

Case History #8: Up, Up and Away

April 8th,2011

The Universe of New 52 Week Highs

The golden week continues as futures soar higher again. The gold futures close at $1,478.40 and silver bumps past the $40 mark to close at $40.60 an ounce.

Gold futures and gold mining stocks are simpatico again. The PHLX Gold/ Silver Index matches new future highs with a new high of 228.95. We don't know it, but this will be a high water mark for the index.

The NYSE flashes eight new highs. They were: Endeavour Silver (EXK 12. 75), Gammon Gold (GDS 10.52), Gold Fields ADS (GFI 18.70), Gold Corp (GG 54.50), Silver Wheaton (SLW 47.60), Silver Corp Metals (SVM 16.32), US Gold Corp (UXG 9.87), and Yamana Gold (AUY 13.40). NYSE Amex has three winners: Capital Gold (CGC 6.57), Central Gold Tr (GTU 55.84), and Extoree Gold Mines (XG 7.80). The NASDAQ has two winners, both silver mining stocks: Pan Am Silver (PAAS 43.06) and Silver Standard (SSRI 35.74).

As usual, the bulk of the universe's winners are from the long ETF family. The new high list included: DBIQ Opt Yld Gold (DGL 51.86), DBIQ Opt Yld Silver (DBS 71.84), ETFS Asian Gold (AGOL 147.24), ETRACS Sil (USV 62.08), ETFS Silver Tr (SIVR 40.61), Glv X Silver Mnr (SIL 31.34), Sprott Physical Silver (PSLV 19.02), iShs Silver Tr (SLV 39.90), iShs Gold Tr (IAU 14.41), Pwr Shs Dbl Gold Long (DGP 45.49), Pro Shs Ult Gold (UGL 75.19), Pro Shs Ult Silver (AGQ 263.74), RBS Trendpilot (TBAR 26.70) and the SPDR Gold Tr (GLD 143.83).

The Universe of New 52 Week Lows

The short side seems to be sensitive to a very small sub set of just four inverse ETFs. We should know these players by heart by now. They were: DUST, DZZ, DGZ and ZSL. Summary

What a phenomenal, incredible, and stupendous week for the long positions in the modern gold trading system. The system should be very easy for you to read by now. I am so happy that I did all this work. The pictures are magnificent!

Case History #9: Gold Takes a Breather

April 12th, 2011

After one of the best weeks in the history of gold and silver, they take a brief vacation. The gold futures fall a modest $14.50 to close at $1,452.90. The silver futures lose a pittance of 55 cents to close at $40.05 an ounce. The PHLX Gold/Silver Index is down 3.98 losing a puny 1.78% for the day. It is a day of small potato losers. In all the universe for gold and silver there are NO new 52 week highs. For the NYSE, the only winner of the day is Newmont Mines NEM) who gains 29 cents for the day when everyone else posts minor negative numbers. It is a day of profit taking and that's what markets are all about.

In a way, I am surprised how sensitive the whole system is to the price of the futures. They are down, but not by much as far as percentages go. It seems to me, the futures act like a light switch. In the ON position, the system lights up in a very predictable manner. In the OFF position like today, the system is completely dark. Is this the end of King Gold and Prince Silver? Is the sky falling? Nope, it is a market trying to establish a trading range. There are not any new lows anywhere in the long side of the system and this is a buying opportunity. The system is running hot and true.

Case History#10: Gold Closes Above $1,500

April 21st, 2011

The Universe of New 52 Week Highs

The month of April has been a defining moment for gold and silver. The futures are trading to new highs. Gold closes above $1,500 an ounce with the futures closing at $1,503.20. Silver has been hotter than gold and the futures close at $46.66 an ounce. While the futures are up, the PHLX Gold/Silver Index fails to keep up the pace. It is up, but no where near it's 52 week high.

The NYSE has just two winners: Barrick Gold (ABX 55.74) and Gold Corp (GG 55.80). There are slim pickings on the NYSE Amex and the NASDAQ with just one winner a piece. For the NYSE Amex it's Extoree Gold (XG 10.08). On the NASDAQ, it's Royal Gold (RGLD 60.74). Royal Gold may be the coolest name in the modern gold trading system?

On the NYSE Arca, there's the cast of usual suspects, a bakers dozen, that seem to be very sensitive to changes in the futures. The winners were: DBIQ Opt Yld Gold (DGL 52.95), DBIQ Opt Yld Silver DBS 81.99), ETFS Asian Gold (SGOL 149.90), ETFS Silver Trust (SIVR 150.69), ETRACS Gold (SGOL 149.90), I Shs Gold (IAU 14.74), I Shs Silver Trust (SLV 46.47), Pwr Shs DB Dbl Gold Long (DGP 47.42), Pro Shs Ult Gold (UGL 78.46), Pro Shs Ult Silver (AGQ 341.50), RBS Trendpilot (TBAR 27.29), Sprott Physical Silver (PSLV 22.50), and the SPDR Gold Tr (GLD 147.06).

The gold mining stocks have lagged with the exception of two at this level. In my universe, for the week, both FrprtMcCG (FCX) and Market Gold Vectors (GDX) were down for the week by more than 6%. The gold mining stocks have come along way and have been prone to profit taking which is a normal event.

NYSE Arca New 52 Week Lows: D

PwrShsDBGold2XShort (DZZ) 6.92, PwrShsDB Gold Short (DGZ) 14.15 and ProShsUltShortSilver (ZSL) 14.74.

The pattern of a series of higher highs for the long side of the gold market and series of lower lows for the short side will be a defining characteristic of the system for the foreseeable future. I think the correlation between new highs in the system and new highs in the futures will be in the high 90's. When the switch is ON for new highs in the futures, the whole system lights up with new highs. Conversely, when the new highs for the futures if OFF, the rest of the system remains dark.

Some Non Random Thoughts

The most important thought I want to share is there isn't any, never was and can't ever be a perfect betting system. Anytime,anyone tries to sell you on the idea that you can win 100% of the time, you need to be on guard. Feelings of invincibility and over confidence are the blind side for the investor even when the odds are on their side.

There are plenty of freak happenings in the modern gold trading system and most of them center around gold mining stocks. On March 30th, 2011 Gold futures were down for the day. Yet two gold mining stocks: Harmony Gold ADS (HMY) on the NYSE and Fronteer Gold (FRG) trading on the NYSE Amex made new 52 week highs. What gives? It's just a hunch but my guess is that some investment firm's research department issued "buy" recommendations for these twins. Both stocks trade around fifteen bucks and spare change and are parts of the PHLX Gold/Silver Stock Index. Using the momentum buy signal of a series of higher highs, I'll bet these two honeys were a "buy" along while back and a lot cheaper. Do I think they aren't buys? No, it just that the Old School of analysis makes them "Johnny Come Latelys."

On April 15th, 2011 gold futures rallied to a settlement high of 1,488.50 and silver futures blasted through 42.56 another new high. The PHLX Gold/Silver Stock Index was down marginally and there were zero new 52 week highs on the NYSE or NASDAQ. The NYSE Amex yielded one new 52 week high, Minoco Gold (MGH) at a price less than a classic cheeseburger. On the other hand, the NYSE Arca showed 13 new 52 week highs with all the usual suspects shinning brightly.

In a big way, the modern gold trading system is the New Age battle between the Old School mode of thinking and the Black Box process of trading. The Old School trades on sentiment, psychology. fundamental analysis and charts. The Black Box is an electro mechanical connection between gold futures and a sub set of ETF's, both long and short. In this fight, I chose the Black Box School of action because they represent a more predictable betting platform. After a long time of looking at data, I think that model will be somewhere near the mid 90% winners, both long and short.

I liked the modern gold trading system because it was easy to decipher, simple to control and effortless to "read." With it's twelve components and more than 100 moveable parts, it was a better choice than the super complex S&P 500 or the even larger monster, the bond system. If you pay attention, the system will tell you what to do. If you take the NYSE part of the systems, count the new 52 week highs as pluses(+), you'll see there is a 100% bias to the buy side for the long position. There are zero new 52 week lows for the NYSE. Right now, the only other system running this "hot" is the oil trading system. Someday, this will all change and the system will tell you when. Even with its limited size, an investor might be bewildered by the many buy choices. I see the multitude of choices as a plus because an investor can match the many different parts to their personality and risk tolerance. Why pay $140 a share when you can buy the same action for $14? Given the wide panorama of choices, maybe the easiest way to reduce the selection process is by price. If you limit your choices to a $20 bet, the world gets smaller; a $15 bet and it gets tiny; at $10 it's skimpy and a five buck or less, it's a downright petite world. A five buck bet or smaller is really a call option without a strike price or expiration date. With a price blow off to the upside near the top, the low price bets have a chance to do very well. At this point, investors will be hunting for anything with the words "gold" or "silver" in it. Watch out for NevGoldRes (UVM) which is a not a gold mining stock but a casino gambling hall.

With the modern gold trading system, it doesn't matter whether gold prices are going up or down according to investment adviser, Mr. Spock, " live long and prosper."

The History of Buy and Sell Signals for Gold Stocks and ETF's 1990-2011

It became very, very clear to me that commodity based stocks like gold and oil, performed significantly differently than their equity based cousins. One of my favorite class of all kinds of stocks has always been oil exploration companies. They would be with me from the beginning in 1975 and be my constant companion. Gold mining stocks made their first appearance in 1990 in my universe. They came and went depending on my level of interest.

Together, oil and gold mining stocks performed significantly lower than other non commodity based stocks in my universe. Without them, the results for the minus method buy signal based on a stock's hyper over sold position, a series of higher new 52 week highs buy signal based on a stock's momentum and the sell signal based on a series of lower new 52 week lows based on momentum would have been much higher. I never considered hiding the results from the 1990's to hype the numbers for non commodity stocks. A good scientist is like a good golfer who plays the ball where it lies. Given a massive data base of over 150,000 numbers, the gold stocks and ETF's were the smallest sub system with an approximate population of 3,500 numbers. Out of that number, about 350 numbers made it as special situations The following is an accurate reflection of gold mining stocks and ETF's special situations, from the latest to oldest.

The data from the modern gold trading system is really the tale of three different cities: Old Town, New Town and Future Town. Old Town started in 1990 and lasted for 19 years. Its inhabitants were all gold mining stocks. Most years there was only a single gold mining stock in Old Town. Once in a while there were two and very rarely (1yr) Old Town was vacant with no gold mining stocks in residence. Those early residents were :ASA, Barrick Gold Mining, Battle Mountain Gold Mining and Homestake Mining. Homestake would be retired to an old folks home when she couldn't put out any more and Battle Mountain would get married in a shot gun wedding. The problem with Old Town was it was too small. With too few residents, it was impossible to generate enough data to build a theory of behavior based on scientific conclusions. Old Town with its small population would yield only observations and semi trends.

New Town was founded in 2009 and was a mix of gold mining stocks and ETF's. It was really the foundation to something bigger, better, and more informative, Future Town. Future Town is the city of tomorrow. Future Town is composed of 100% ETF's, matched (long v short) and few leveraged. There are five sets of ETF twins living in Future Town. I believe they will yield the data over time to build a conclusive theory about the modern gold trading system.

Old Town and New Town would generate a lot of food for thought. Things to chew on were that ETF's were significantly more predictable than gold mining stocks alone. There was a definite pattern of behavior in the combined two towns. Inhabitants who were identified as hyper over sold were clearly superior to their other family members. The poorest performers were gold mining stocks making new 52 week lows. It was diabolical because rather than going down in price they had a strong tendency to go up. Gold mining stocks making new 52 week highs were a good news-bad news scene. They were uneven performers. It is time to take a closer look at the performance of the three cities, starting with the Old Town, first built in 1990.

1990 was just like a huge punch to my gut with everything I had learned since 1985 put in jeopardy. ASA flashed three buy signals with the trusted minus method in the same year resulting in a train wreck of losses. This pattern never showed its ugly mug again in the next twenty years in any part of the bigger system. In 1990, gold prices began an extended bear market when central banks around the world started to sell mountains of gold. What originally appeared to be a short term over sold gold mining stock prices cascaded into a series of lower and lower prices. The losses of 1990 would taint the whole system at large and depressed its results for a very long time. I lost my lust for gold mining stocks for quite some time after 1990. It was a real temptation to dump gold mining stocks forever.

The next six years produced a mixed bag of results with the prices of gold being pretty crazy and the results were skewed to the negative side. 1997saw a unique two "false positives" in the same year for gold mining stock, Home Stake(HM). HM was heading towards oblivion and maybe this was the stock's first hint of troubles to come? I'd abandon HM from my universe at this point. Adios, old friend. In 1999, I'd see something that only happened one other time in the larger universe. It was a stock making one new 52 week high with no second confirming "buy" signal in the same calendar year. Let this be a lesson to eager traders who want to jump the gun and get into a stock early that's making new 52 week highs. To add salt to the wound, the stock was one of my favorites,ABX! In late 2004, there was a seismic shift in the data for gold mining stocks and ETF's. It may have been an interaction between an almost linear, straight up increase in gold prices and the introduction of new ETF's directly linked to gold bullion prices? Whatever, the data went from being the dunce of the class to super star performer and gave the numbers a new lease on life .Between 2004 and 2011, winners beat losers by a 21 to 5 count or 80% more closely replicating the results of the over all larger universe of stocks. Before you break out your checkbook with reckless abandon here is something to think about. The over all numbers from 1990 to 2011 are an unacceptable bet. My bare minimum to even consider making a bet is a 50/50 chance of winning. It is what it is and the collective aggregate of data gives us a chance with a 47% win chance over a 21 year period. Is the glass half empty or half full? Does10 years of pain offset 10 years of gain? Does the fundamental change in the structure of the system in late 2004 outweigh the previous 10 years of numbers. I think so, but to err on the side of safety, if you want to join the band of gold profit seekers, maybe the best bet is a non gold mining ETF. Data from 2012 and the first six months of 2013 would push the ratio of winners versus loser over the 50% winners hump. This was due to the near 100% reliability of long and short gold bullion ETFs.

Gold Prices

So what makes the day to day world wide gold trading system work? At the electronic heart of the market is the constant pulse of changing gold prices. It's tough to catalog all the reasons that gold prices go up and down. Some day's it's supply and demand. Other day's, it's greed and fear or fear and greed. It's unregulated hedge funds, derivatives and market manipulation. The centerpieces are a near pornographic US dollar lows and obscenely low interest rates. It's fifteen million Americans out of work and huge deficits . It's a massive trade imbalance with Red China. It's visions of the threat of oil supply disruptions, civil unrest in the Middle East, and rumors of war. It's the fury of Mother Nature unleashing floods, earth quakes and tsunamis. What's worse, four leaking nuclear reactors in Japan or mountains of sovereign debt in Europe? The latest bogey-man in the game is rising inflation, a longtime soul mate of gold. It's a cornucopia of reasons with different combinations being the stars of the day. And then there is politics. The modern gold bull market began in 2000 with the election of George Bush as the 43rd President of the US. The exact date of the beginning of the beginning was November 17th, 2000 and the world would never be the same. Just after his election in 2000 and before his inauguration, investor's began to dump US dollars and buy gold. The ten year gold bear market was over. Was it the election of George Bush or the end of the decade long massive selling by central banks of physical stocks of gold? It was probably a little of both, but one thing is certain, no one could have ever predicted how poorly the US dollar would fare under the stewardship of President George Bush, Number 43.

In 2002, I began collecting news articles following the ups and downs of gold. I was looking for a central theme to explain gold price fluctuations and my narrative starts with Matt Kranz of USA Today, "Gold rush could signal trouble," May 10th,2002. Gold was peaking at a new high of $309.50 per ounce, up nearly 90% from November,2000. Gold mining stocks are trading at new two year new highs as tech stocks along with the over all markets are plunging. Looking back, it may well be a hangover from Enron, World.Com and the Dot. Com disaster? Matt Kranz also points to rising oil prices, fears of inflation and worries about tensions in the Middle East " Most important, the weakening US dollar is causing nervous investor's to buy gold for safety." My hat is off to JamesDines who closes the article by declaring, " It's a bull market for gold." In a world of mealy mouthed, weak sister recommendations, it was cool to see one person really step up.

According to the writing duo of John Waggoner and Sue Kirchoff of USA Today in November 2003, fears about global unrest fuel a buying spree in gold. " Gold rocketed to a 7 ½ year high Wednesday fueled by the falling dollar and global unrest." Gold soared to $394.50 an ounce and was up nearly 14% for the year. " Investor's flock to gold when the value of the US dollar falls on world currency markets." On Wednesday, it took $1.16 to buy a euro against $1.15 on Tuesday. Considering it took a $1.05 to buy a euro at the beginning of the year, it's easy to see the appeal of gold. Gold like oil is priced in US dollars. " When the US currency weakens, that makes gold less costly on foreign markets to foreign investors," concludes Alex Beuzelein, senior marker analysts at Ruesch International. I wonder, how far down the Rolodex did they go to find this guy?

In early December 2003, gold prices rose $5.90 an ounce to close at $402.70. It punched through the $400 an ounce barrier and reached its highest price since 1996. This will be the first time, financial writers will describe gold as a "safe haven" investment. The dollar has declined 10% against the euro and the yen for the year. Scandals at US mutual fund companies along with low interest rates continue to pump gold prices higher.

Nearly a month later, gold prices rose to $424.40 an ounce and silver was up 28 cents to $6.23, the highest level in five years. The dollar weakened to set a new record of $1.27 per euro and fell flat on its face against the yen. It is positively sickening to watch the dollar's slide, but this is just the beginning.

Toward the end of 2004, gold prices were bumping up near the $450 mark, a 16 year high. According to Michael Cuggino, manager of the Permanent Portfolio Fund, " Low short term interest rates, the decreasing dollar, the unstable situation in the Middle East, the war on terrorism, the overall feeling of instability-these are all the things that move people toward gold." Milton Ezrati, senior economic and market strategist at money management firm, Lord Abbett tells investors to think twice before investing in gold because, "they've already missed the boat." He feels the US dollar is poised to rebound, causing gold prices to fall. He further cautions against owning gold and oil at the same time. " If you have oil stocks or other price sensitive or inflation sensitive commodity stocks, you could wind up doubling your bet and not be aware of it." Stupid, stupid, stupid investors, own gold and oil at the same time, how dumb can you be?

Toward the end of 2004, gold prices begin to fall as a stronger US dollar, fund selling, month end book squaring and stop loss orders rule the day. Gold fell by $8.30 an ounce to close at its lowest level in twelve days. OMG, the sky is falling, it's the end of the world! Really, the end of the world? This is the normal price movement for any investment that is seeking to establish a trading range. These dips are buying opportunities, not selling decisions.

As 2004 turns into 2005, gold prices continue to slide as the US dollar gains against the euro. On January 8th, 2005, gold is off $2.10 to close at $418.90, down from its 04 high of $453.40 on November 30th. LF "Sonny" Davidson, an Edward Jones financial adviser predicts gold prices "will hover around $400 to $430, but if demand kicks up, certainly the price will rise. Last year, I didn't think it would reach $400." When gold punched through $500, the paper would again turn to "Sonny" for his opinion and he would have a melt down moment. In so many words, he tells the residents of Elko that he hated gold stocks because they were speculative. The only way he would sell them is if a customer held a gun to his head. He also informed the press, he worked for a "conservative" firm. Conservative is code for mutual funds and bonds. Given that two of the largest US gold mining firms, Newmont Mines (NEM) and Barrick Gold (ABX) were fifty miles down I-80, it may not have been the PR Edward Jones was looking for. After that, I never heard another peep from "Sonny" about gold prices again. I wonder, who called his bosses, Newmont or Barrick? It was probably both!

It wasn't that I lost interest in gold and silver, but in a way, it was boring because the message was always the same. As gold jumped through $500, $600,$700,$800, and $900 an ounce, it was the falling US dollar, fears of inflation, deficits, unrest in the Middle East, ad nauseam, and ad infinitum. For the naysayers, the price was too high and for the bulls, it was too low. 2008 was a terrible year for retail investors, one of the most horrible since the 1930's. On one of the most gruesome trading days in history, Friday October 10th, the NYSE recorded 2,901 new 52 week lows and a paltry 10 new 52 week highs. On the NASDAQ, there were 1,514 new 52 week lows and one, lone, solitary new 52 week high, Royal Gold (RGLD) at $40.94 a share. In a frightful year for stocks, gold will punch through $1,000 an ounce and hit its 2008 high of $1,011 in April.

In 2009, gold gained 32%, closing at a record $1,141 an ounce on Thursday, November 19th, 2009. However, the biggest star of 09 was silver, up 71% and gaining momentum like a runaway freight train. The fuel was the same, fears of a lower US dollar and rising inflation.

Wednesday, September 2010 sees gold rising $24.60 an ounce to $1,269.70 on the Comex. "Safe haven (gold) demand is continuing, as there are increasing doubts about the robustness of the recent economic recovery and concerns that markets may be subject to further turmoil," said Mark O'Bryne, director for Dublin bullion dealer, Gold Core. Bullion is up 16% for the year and the latest jumps feeds the bulls who argue that the negative effects of government spending on currency will propel gold to $1,600 an ounce and beyond.

On November 9th, 2010 gold prices close above $1,400 for the first time caused by uncertainty on the outcome of the Group of 20 currency meetings and worries about sovereign debt in Europe. " Gold's rally won't end before the metal hits $1,500 this year. But when it does run out of gas, the crash will probably be hard," said Craig Ross, VP of Chicago brokerage ApexFutures.com.

On April 6th,2011, financial writer Tatyana Shumsky of the WSJ writes, "Gold pushed further into record territory as renewed inflation and sovereign debt default spurred investment demand for safe harbor assets." The price of gold settled at $1,485.80 an ounce on the COMEX. " Assuming investment demand at some point takes off again this year, there remains good scope for new highs to be recorded," states metals consultant, GPMS, Ltd.

Investor's stampeded into the arms of the safety of gold and silver after monthly data showed China's CPI vaulted to 5.4%. The US government rigs it's inflation numbers by excluding energy and food to continue keeping interest rates artificially low. The true measure of US inflation may be the massive amounts of dollars the US prints every 24 hours. "Investors are frustrated with US monetary policy. They're saying the heck with the dollar and their buying metals," said Ira Epstein, director of the Ira Epstein division of the Linn Group.

The final word goes to Carolyn Cui of the WSJ, " Gold continued its upward march in a time of global financial tumult, closing above $1,500 an ounce Thursday for the first time as investors seek safe heaven in the metal." This nearly identical to Tatyana Shumsky's opening exactly one week earlier. The problem with repeating the same thing day after day is readers begin to believe it's all true. Gold as a safe haven, safe harbor is becoming a mantra, a very dangerous mantra. "The reason for gold's ability to do well in any market lies in its role as a haven from concerns about the dollar, inflation and shocks in Europe, the Middle East, and Japan," writes Cui. She furthers states, " Gold is seen as a lasting store of value, which doesn't erode like that of currencies." I wonder if Ms. Cui was even born in the mid 80's, when gold suddenly lost its "lasting store of value"?

From the beginning of the run up in gold starting on February 17th, 2000 to the high water mark of over $1,500, there has been one central theme: abnormally low interest rates causing the pummeling of the US dollar. For eight years, the US dollar suffered at the hands of President George Bush, the 43rd. Under his leadership the US went from surplus to massive deficits, from lender to borrower and from boom to bust. The US dollar has fared just as poorly under the leader- ship of President Barrack Obama. It made me ill to watch the once mighty US dollar slide versus the euro, sick to experience the downfall of the dollar against the yen, and positively nauseous over the dollars crash against the Mexican Peso. The winners of this long descent into financial insanity were the big spenders in Washington DC and their pay masters on Wall Street. The big losers were Grandma and Grandpa who saw interest rates on their savings accounts crash to nothing while prescription drug prices, medical care, gas and food went up. The old and the middle class have been getting squeezed. You want to know why gold is sky high? It's because the value of the US dollar is so low making it little better than the currency of some third world Banana Republic.

The second theme throughout gold's ten year bull market is it's value as a safe haven or safe harbor asset. Answers.com defines safe haven as " the action of investors moving their capital away from riskier investments to the safest possible investment vehicles. This flight is usually caused by uncertainty in the financial or international markets." Gold is not, never has been and never will be a safe haven investment. For me, "safe haven" is a marketing word and not quantifiable like " low interest rates" or the "falling dollar." Selling investors on the idea that gold is a safe haven investment is like marketing a pit bull having the personality of a border collie. The true character of gold is one of extreme violence and any thoughts that it is in any way benign can only bring heart break.

The End Game

The one grand view that I have of all markets, after nearly forty years of observation, is that they are cyclical. Nothing goes up forever and every investment dog has its day. After a decade of falling gold prices (bear market), gold is moving toward the eleventh year of ever increasing gold prices (bull market). I think the bull still has legs. The current bull market in gold will have an end game just like every "bubble" before it. According to financial writer Robert Blumen on May 29th 2010, " Respected value investor Jeremy Grantham 'guarantees' that gold will crash.' I hate gold, it does not pay a dividend, it has no value and you can't work out what it should or shouldn't be worth… it is the last refuge of the desperate." I don't understand the venom and I don't put much stock in open end prophesies like Mr. Grantham's. When gold crashes and it will, Mr.

Grantham will have his "I told you so" moment. While his forecast sounds authoritative, it does little to help the average Joe Blow in Normal, Illinois.

Well, Mr. Joe B., there will be at least six signals the bull market in gold is over and a new cycle is beginning. Just like the bull market start on November 17th,2000, the beginning of the end or the start of the bear will be an after the fact, historical call. On the other hand, if you are paying attention to the world around you, there's a very good chance, you can catch the turn. If you are oblivious to world events, you are going to get caught with your knickers down.

At the pinnacle of gold's ascent, silver will over take gold as the darling of the investment world. Because gold is so expensive, silver will appear to be cheap. There will be lines at pawnshops as people sell grandma's sterling silver set they got as a wedding present and longer lines at coin shops as others load up on silver coins, the true last refuge of the desperate. A blow up in silver will signal the demise of gold.

The next clue the bull market is over will be the complete absence of new 52 week highs throughout the entire gold trading system. Once where there were bright lights, it will be completely dark. The cause of the change will be falling gold future prices. How will you know if this is a whipsaw, just a new trading range or the real deal of a new cycle? One of the reasons I like my system is that is so visual. The new cycle will look like someone walking down a flight of stairs. The weekly highs will be lower and lower until they disappear. One thing I like to do is to look back and find the previous weekly lowest low and when weekly highs trade below that number, I'm starting to think new cycle. The traditional way of determining a new bear market is when prices fall 20% from their high water mark. Of course, for the most conservative of investors, the clearest signal of the bear market is when inverse ETF's start making new 52 week highs and the long ETF's start making new 52 week lows.

Next will be the driving force behind lower gold future prices, rising interest rates. The US will fight the tide of rising interest rates tooth and nail, but in the end, will be forced to follow the lead of the rest of the world. If the US had it's druthers, they'd keep interest rates at new zero for as long as possible. Given the sheer magnitude of US debt, even the smallest interest rate increases are going to force the US to pony up significantly more dough to service the debt. It's an economy killer, means less in the way of services for everyone, and will force some pretty ugly political choices. Events, half way around the world in Red China, may well be the catalyst for the bear markets in the US.

Since 2000, we have seen the direct influence that interest rates have on the price of gold. In a brilliant piece of analysis, CPA Adam Hamilton (no relation) traces the route of negative interest rates and the rising prices of gold. How can I have a negative return when I have a positive yield? If you take today's return of .20% for a 1 yr US T bill , bought at a discount 999.80 and redeem it at par, 100(1000) and then subtract the current inflation rate plus federal income taxes, you are losing at least $3.00 of purchasing power for every $100! Negative returns on debt are the prime factor in forcing investor's into the loving arms of commodities speculation.

The last time interest rates were positive was back in 2001 when gold was bumbling along in the mid $250's an ounce. Will rising interest rates guarantee lower gold prices? I think in the beginning, it will be some what uneven. I remember the late 70' and early 80's when rising interest rates were dwarfed by even higher rates of inflation. Over time, as world interest rates ramp up, the US will be forced to play a game they don't want and can't win, playing catch up. It won't be until interest rates turn positive will investor's dump gold for the real purchasing power of debt. And that my friends, might take years.

I was born a contrarian and by the age of six, I was a dyed in the wool cynic. At twelve, I was a committed anarchist devoted to the destruction of the status quo. I have never, ever been a fan of consensus thinking. I refuse to follow the beat of the Old School drummer.

A huge signal of a gold market top will be a consensus among all the experts, real and imagined, that gold can't possibly be at a top. Gold will be universally loved, except by a few hum bugs, and the experts will select some outrageous consensus number. The NUMBER will be a sound bite that echos throughout the electronic media. The NUMBER will be a song at parties and it will the anthem of the financial services industry. What had been too risky at $1,000 an ounce will suddenly be a steal at two times or more as much! Why? It's because investor's will have sold themselves on gold at the top and financial adviser's always do what's easy rather than what is right. The financial services industry is so committed to consensus behavior that they are a prime example of what sociologist Irving Janus calls "group think." Group think is the ultimate form of consensus behavior, no deviates allowed in this system. At the end game, the talking heads will all agree that it will be impossible for gold to go down.

Last time, at the top of the gold price roller coaster there was a mania for gold coins. The number one gold bullion coin in the last bull market cycle was the South African Krugerrand. For investors, at the top, gold coins will be en vogue and the rage of the system. A note of caution, it took all the suckers who bought Krugerrands at the last top, nearly a quarter of a century to get back to even. Not the best of news for someone is their sixties. You can spot a gold market ultimate high when dear old Dad trades his muni bonds for gold bullion coins. The second Grandma sells her utility stocks to buy gold American Eagles, it is time to jump ship.

The signals that gold's bull is dying will come from around the planet. The world wide focal point for civil unrest and riots will be the Gold Exchange in Mumbai, India. A major part of the economic fabric of India is the use of gold as collateral for all kinds of business ventures. When gold prices are at their peak, the counter parties will refuse to deliver their pledged gold to fulfill their contract's. The result will be very violent with accounts settled with guns, knives, and fists. In India, blood will be the means of settling gold accounts, and it will definitely be a world wide news event.

Finally, the last piece of the mosaic will be the smallest and most subtle part of the larger picture. The last spasm of the gold bull market will be an explosion of "cheap" gold mining stocks sold on the Toronto Stock Exchange (TSE). Investor's who couldn't find Toronto on a map will be rabid fans of a $4 a share last chance at gold glory.

In summary, there is an end game for the gold bull market because it is an inevitable part of the cycle of ups and downs. A fair question is where do I think the top of the market is? So far, we have smashed through the old all time price high of the last cycle of $875 and have nearly doubled that previous bench mark. I believe, in order to complete the new cycle, gold will have to penetrate the old inflationary high's equivalent of more than $2,000 an ounce. With gold trading currently in a tight range of $1,500 an ounce, the possibility of gold advancing another $500 is very real. After that, we are in uncharted territory. Just like all previous bubbles, there will be panic buying at the top, an orgy of excess, and feelings of euphoric over confidence. All the while, there will be a conspiracy of signals of a coming gold collapse and the beginning of a new bear market cycle. The seven signals of the beginning of the end of the bull market cycle will be: silver will trump gold as investor's favorite hole card, a sudden absence of new 52 week highs in the system, a change in the direction of interest rates, a universal consensus that gold can't miss and prices are going higher, a mania for gold bullion coins, disruption of the Mumbai gold market, and a plethora of speculative gold mining stocks on the Toronto Stock Exchange. Peter Cooper says, " George Soros got it right recently when he said gold was the 'ultimate bubble,' that is to say the last asset in the chain to become a bubble before the whole cycle starts again." Maybe, Grantham was right, "gold is the last refuge of the desperate"?

So the bubble explodes and blows up in everyone's face. So what? The next phase of the bubble, the crash, may be one of the best money making opportunities of your life. This wasn't just another book about how to make money when gold prices go up, but a vision on how to profit when gold prices crash.

The investor's who will be under the most stress are those who bought at the pinnacle of gold prices. They will be in a state of psychological shock and emotional stress. These are not the best conditions to making big decisions, but they have choices to make. Typically, the first response is to do nothing and hope for the best. After losing so much money, they toss in the towel, surrender to the bear and watch their money evaporate. We have been conditioned to accept losses and it's become part of our investment DNA to let our losses run. It's a pity, but it seems the investment world has forgotten the prime directive of the preservation of capital. So, the money tide has turned against you, what comes next? If you were lucky and made a bundle on the way up, it's time to take profits. If you bought at the top, it's time to preserve your capital. Any way you slice the Jarlsberg cheese, it's time to SELL!

Here's the really cool thing, if you never bet on the rise of gold, you can make as much or more on its fall. If you were a winner on the way up, you can be an even bigger winner on the way down. All it takes is a different kind of mindset that when things go from bad to worse, you can win big.

Forget about puts or short sales, the key to winning big on gold's fall is the inverse ETF. As the price of gold decreases, the value of an inverse ETF will increase. The following is a glimpse of the future. On April 12th, 2011 gold prices were under pressure as the precious metal was seeking to establish the bottom of a new trading range. The price of gold fell by $14.50 an ounce.

ETF	$Gain/(Loss)	%Gain/(Loss)
NUGT	(-1.29)	
DUST(short)	+1.30	
DGP		(-1.41)
DZZ (short)		+1.49

This is a world of harmony, symmetry, balance and congruency. It's a universe of predictability where there are no ugly, stab you in the back behaviors. If you need a mental picture of how these matched long and short ETF's work, take two glasses, fill them half full of water, and everyday pour water in even amounts from one glass to the other. It is the back and forth transfer of money between the long and short ETF's that make them so incredibly valuable.

For three days, May 3rd to the 5th, gold and silver got hammered to the downside. The selling pressure reached an apex on Friday, the 5th with gold down $34 an ounce and silver tumbling $3.15 an ounce. The metals had been over bought on the short term and trader's were dumping silver because it's margin rates had been raised three days in a row. Another factor hurting the metals was a huge rally in the US dollar which forced commodities across the board lower.

ETF	$Gain/(Loss)	%Gain/(Loss)
NUGT	(-2.56)	-7.46
DUST (short)	+3.12	+7.60
AGQ	(-54.86)	-23.42
ZSL (short)	+4.89	+25.14
DGP	(-2.98)	-6.25
DZZ (short)	+.39	+5.64

Some day, when the gold bear emerges from her den, the four most valuable asset choices in the investment galaxy will be inverse ETF's. My favorite four, in order of preference are: Pro Share Ult Short Silver (ZSL), DIREXIONDAILYGOLDMINER'SBEAR 3XShares(DUST), Pro Shares DB Gold Double Short (DZZ) and finally, Pro Shares DB Gold Short ETN (DGZ).

ZSL wins first place because in the last crash of silver prices, the silver bullion fell by nearly 50% in less than a week. If you catch the ZSL wave at the right time, it could be one of the best sets in your life. I favor DUST in second because when gold prices break, investor's will dump gold mining shares with a vengeance. Gold mining stock's will shed value like a 500 lb giant on the "Biggest Loser" and DUST will be the biggest winner. At the lower end of choices, I prefer the leverage advantage that DZZ enjoys over DGZ.

There is a bad news, good news scenario for calling the turn of the gold and silver markets from bull to bear. The bad news is that none of the experts are going to tell you about the turn. It just isn't in their DNA. Jim and Chuck won't.

Their expert pals will tell you to stand pat and do nothing. The money honey babes who read the teleprompter on TV can't because they are clueless.

The really good news is you can make the call by yourself. Just remember, you don't have to be a weather expert to know the wind is blowing 50 MPH. You don't need a MBA from Wharton to know what a minus sign means. You don't need a PhD from the University of Oregon in economics to know what 52 week new lows and new 52 week highs signify. All you have to do is learn to trust that little voice in your head.

It doesn't matter any more that things can go from bad to worse, the world of inverse ETF's means you can profit from any disaster. There is a silver lining to the upcoming drop in gold prices and it's the chance to be a winner rather than a loser. The key is to build your self confidence that you can profit when things turn gold into pewter. It just isn't the precious metals, but there's a disaster brewing in stocks and bonds. These disasters will provide a golden opportunity for the inverse world of ETF's to shine. When everything turns into an ugly can of worms, when it comes to inverse ETF's, it's better to be just a tad early, rather than too late, or even worse, not at all.

The Gospel of Selling Covered Calls

If I had only one hour left in my life and had a choice to speak on any investment topic, I'd use it to spread the gospel of selling covered calls. The good news about selling covered calls is an investor can turn any non income producing asset stock or ETF into a cash cow.

Before we look at why we should sell covered calls AKA writing options, we need a short review of the basics of an options contract. Every listed options contract has four parts: contract size, the expiration date, the strike price, and the premium. Three parts of the contract are standardized: size, expiration, and strike prices. Only the premium will change minute by minute as the price of the underlying asset changes minute by minute. The correlation between the under- lying asset and the premium is an astounding .999!

Every contract requires a minimum of one round lot or 100 shares per contract. If you own 872 shares of an optionable stock, you can sell (write) eight contracts. Conversely, if you own 82 shares of stock, you will have to buy an additional 18 shares to be able to sell one contract. The expiration date is a fixed date on the calendar. When the contracts expire, it's game over. There are many expiration dates to choose from giving an investor a high degree of flexibility. The final part of the standardized contract is the strike price. This is the amount that the seller (you) agrees to accept for the sale of your stock. The premium is the amount of money the seller (you) receive for agreeing to sell your stock at a specified price (expiration date) for a specific price(strike price). The premium belongs to the seller and is yours to keep no matter what happens next. The value of the premium is based on two factors. First is the relationship between the underlying asset and the strike price. If the underlying asset is below the strike price, it's out of the money., and if the underlying asset is above the strike price it's in the money. My life revolves around out of the money calls. Second is time to contract expiration. Usually, the longer the time to expiration, the bigger the premium. If you sell call options, time is your friend and if you buy calls, time is your enemy. Once when you see how all four parts interact, you will see a true ballet where all the parts work in concert.

I can't even think of a more conservative way to make money and maybe that's the big problem. In a game where investor's have been brainwashed into thinking they are home run hitters and have to swing for the fences every time they are at bat, it's tough to convince them to play differently. It's extremely difficult to sell something that a dog trot jog into second for a stand up double should be a part of their game plan. Who wants to swing a bat like Wade Boggs or Rod Carew when they see themselves as Barry Bonds, Hank Aaron or the Bambino? An investor who sells covered calls rarely strikes out, has an incredible on base average, but doesn't rate much of the way of headlines on ESPN. Selling covered calls have three big benefits: the creation of income, the locking in of profits, and giving themselves some measure of downside protection.

The Case for Barrick Gold Mining (ABX)

I am not by nature a very sentimental man. I don't fall in love easily and tend to view investments with a distant detachment. They are just numbers in a long succession of numbers. But, when it comes to Barrick Gold Mining (ABX), I do have a soft spot in my heart for them.

First, over a twenty year period, I collected more data on ABX than any other gold mining stock. Next, for three years I delivered parts to Barrick Gold Strike in the Carlin Trend. I got to know the people who worked at Gold Strike up close and personal. From the administrative office in Elko, to all the different warehouses (particularly the Mieckle gang), and all the professional staff, they were a terrific group to work with. I can't recall a single bad word or negative attitude any where in the whole organization during my tenure.

The reason I respect Barrick Gold Strike was their commitment to the safety of all personnel who worked on the property. A lot of firms give you a wink and a nod when it comes to safety. At Barrick Gold Strike it was part of the corporate DNA. Everyone, from big shot executives to the janitor was held accountable when it came to safety. Working below ground is a tough, dirty and dangerous job. If some kid told me they wanted to be a miner, I'd say go to work for Barrick Gold Strike.

For most investors, it comes down to the fundamentals when making a decision to buy a stock. The following is a Kodak snapshot for the fundamentals for ABX on Friday, July 20,2012. The current yield was 2.30% with a P/E of 7.67. At this point, ABX looks more like a utility equity than a gold mining stock.

There's a trap that declining stocks all have. As the price plummets, the current yield goes up and the P/E goes down. You have to be very, very careful. The last time I got tricked by this illusion was when a stock fundamentally had triple fives: $ 5 price (cheap), 5% dividend (big money) and a P/E of 5. That stock was Poloroid (PRD) on its way to bankruptcy and a valuation of zero! **I made a hard and fast rule right then and there. Never, ever buy anything making new 52 week LOWS.**

ABX is coming off a devastating series of new 52 week lows. There was nothing fundamentally wrong with ABX. It was all a cyber attack by short sellers. There was some fallout for ABX as they fired their CEO for falling stock prices. That was like shooting the pig when it was the rooster who gave you the flu.

ABX is making money on its gold operations. It has stopped making new 52 week lows and fundamentally looks like a conservative buy. Its future looks bright. There is one big negative in its future and that's the price of copper. The fact that copper prices are weak spells big troubles for the bigger economy.

Where can you find data about premiums, expiration dates and strike prices? You can use IBD, the only daily financial paper that carries intel on options. My vision is so poor, it's really tough for me to see the very small numbers anymore. I prefer Yahoo! because I can blow up the screen and the following numbers came from July 20th when ABX closed at $34.57 a share.

Cash flow is measured by dividing the premium by the purchase price of ABX. On July 20th, I looked at the August, October and January calls which expired on the 11th day of each month. I further chose the strike prices of 37 and 38.

August 37	October 37	January 37
.43	$1.22	$2.14
divided into	divided into	divided into
$34.57=	$34.57 =	$34.57=
.01%	3.5%	6%
August 38	October 38	January 38
$ .24= .006%	.92= 2.7%	$ 2.14= 5.3%

If your contracts expire worthless and are unexercised and this is the ball game. In a world of low dividend paying stocks and the lowest interest rates for over forty years, selling calls creates cash flow. As you can see, time is the name of the game with the 37's ranging from .01 to 6% and the 38's paying out .006% to 5.3%. It might seem like chump change, but a .01 mirrors short term bank CDs and 6% beats just about everything. And never forget, the .01% was earned in thirty days, not a year. The upper range of the income stream of 5.3% to 6% beats the living stuffing out of 30 year T Bonds by a better than 2 to 1 margin. 30 years or 90 days, which one appeals to you?

Locking in Profits

A lot of investors never make any money because they never sell at a profit. Selling covered calls will force you to take a profit. To calculate the amount of the locked in profit, add the premium to the amount you win by subtracting the purchase price of ABX from the strike price. So if you subtract $34.57 from 37.00 (strike price) you have a gain of $2.43 a share and for the 38's, you win $3.43 per share. This is the profit you receive if the contract is exercised by the buyer.

August 37	October 37	January 37
$ .43+$2.43=$2.86	$1.22+$2.43=$3.65	$2.14+$2.43
8.3%	10.6%	13.2%
August 38	October 38	January 38
$.24+$3.43=$4.69	$.92+$3.43=$4.35	$1.85+$3.43=$5.28
10.6%	12.5%%	15.3%

These are the maximum gains for a seller of ABX covered calls. It's a curse and a blessing depending on your point of view. It's a curse because that's all there is. It's a blessing because you made a profit. I am going out on a limb, but I'm don't think the S&P 500 index will do any better for the year. It is what it is, a double and it never will be a home run .

Breaking Even and Downside Protection

The premium acts as a cushion against downside price action. Simply, take the price of the underlying asset ABX and subtract the premium you received and that's your downside protection. You won't lose a penny until the underlying assets price passes below that number.

August 37	October 37	January 37
$34.57-$ .43=$34.87	$34.57-$1.22=$33.53	$34.57-$2.14=$32.43
August 38	October 38	January 38
$34.57-$.24=$34.23	$34.57-$.92=$33.65	$34.57-$1.85=$32.73

Breaking even on the upside is taking the premium and adding it to the strike price. You won't lose any money until the price of ABX passes through that number. The break evens will define your investment and should be calculated before you ever sell a call. If you don't like the range of the break evens, don't do the deed.

August 37	October 37	January 37
37+$.43=$37.43	37+$1.22=$38.22	37+$2.14=$39.14
August 38	October 38	January 38
38+$.24=$38.24	38+$1.22=$39.22	38+$1.85=$39.85

We now have our break evens for the downside and upside. It's elementary school math. It's too bad that brokers are too lazy to do it. You don't need a degree in mathematics from California State University to figure all this out. Shopping around for commissions is very smart because they do impact rates of return.

Selling calls isn't for everyone. First, if you have a deep emotional or extreme attachment to your stocks, don't sell covered calls. For some investors, losing their beloved stocks can be very painful. Maybe, Grandpa gave them the stocks or they worked their entire life for the same company and accumulated them as a retirement package. Always remember, when you sell covered calls, you stand a chance of losing your stocks through exercise. If you are in the money, say bye bye to your stock. It's a goner for sure.

Second, if you have a very low cost basis stock, you should be exceptionally careful about selling calls. So, if you own Microsoft (MSFT) with a cost basis of $5 a share, an exercise call at any price could trigger a huge tax bite from Uncle Sammy. If your tax liability is larger than your projected returns, don't do the deed. I liked to use low cost basis stock in a margin account as collateral to buy stocks that I could safely sell calls against.

Finally, if you fret about leaving any money on the table, selling calls is not your cup of mocha. Sometimes, a stock will blow right through your strike price, fly past your break even and keep on going. The absolute worst case scenario is if someone makes a hostile bid for your stock and if you sold calls, you are going to leave a lot of dough on the table. Some people equate leaving money on the table with "losing money" and it makes them very angry. If you aren't happy with the pre-defined risks and returns, don't do the deed.

With so many choices between expiration dates and strike prices, where do you start? Most rookies are going to go as far out on the calendar as possible. In looking at ABX I didn't even consider the January 2012 calls. Rooks generally go for the longest distance for strike prices. I never pick a strike price higher than the previous new 52 week high and like strike prices that hover near returning me 10%. Long distance expiration dates and strike prices are not the worst strategy in the world, but I like a different game. Out of all the choices, I liked the Oct 37 and 38 calls the most. They appeal to me because I want near instant gratification, love money I can make sooner than later, and I really want the chance to write calls three times or more a year. There is a benefit for January calls. The taxes aren't due until April of the next year.

What happens if the price of ABX goes down? You can buy back the calls at a significantly lower price and re write the position at a lower strike price. The goal is to always be making income and the more premiums you collect, the lower your risk of ownership in the investment.

Selling covered calls is a good idea for investor's who need income. With historic low interest rates, anemic CD's, and dwarf size stock dividends, people need every dime that can get just to get by. Selling covered calls just might be the difference you need in cash flow needed to make your life a little more manageable.

Selling covered calls may well help solve the horrific problem of what to do about capital loss carry forwards? Retail investors have been raped for years by the Federal government when it comes to the tax treatment of capital losses. The $3,000 limit of offsetting losses with ordinary income is older than the hills. This sickening figure should have been indexed all along. This insult should be at least $30,000 a year. As it stands, an investor with six figure capital losses, can be forced to string those losses out for decades. The beauty of selling covered calls is the profits from exercising the contract are taxed as short term capital gains and be used to off set capital losses on a dollar for dollar basis. So a $2.43 short term capital gain looks more attractive when it's used to off set a $2.43 of accumulated capital losses. When it comes to the horror of capital losses, don't get mad, get even and selling calls can help you do that.

Finally, someday when the price of gold and silver collapses, and inverse ETF's are making new 52 week highs, selling covered calls will create cash flow, lock in profits, and provide downside protection. Maybe, just maybe, 1 in a 100,000 retail brokers are any good at selling covered calls. **For most investors, this is a do it on your own strategy.** In proofing this section, I should have never broken the prime directive of buying anything making new 52 week lows. Between then and now, ABX would lose 50% of its market value.

Gold Prices Go Nuclear

When it comes to investing, school is never out of session. There are no spring breaks or summer vacation. If you ever stop learning, you are missing new opportunities to be earning. For investors, if you snooze, you lose and that's why I love it all so much. It is a never ending learning experience, a curriculum in a constant state of change, and two days are rarely the same. Since the last case history when gold closed above $1,500 an ounce there have been some new important lessons to be learned. After gold punched past $1,500 , a lot of things happened. From those events, there were four new lessons and one new important addition to the larger gold trading system.

After gold whizzed through $1,500, it looked like gold was a runaway freight train, rumbling to a breath taking series of higher highs. It was momentum on steroids.

The Gold Express:

Date	New 52 Week High
4/25	1,508.60 U
4/27	1,516.70 U

4/28	1,530.80 U
4/29	1.556.00 U
7/12	1,562.30 U
7/13	1,585.20 U
7/14	1,592.80 U
7/18	1,602.40 U
7/25	1,612.00 U
7/26	1,616.60 U
7/29	1,628.30 U
8/2	1,641.90 U
8/8	1,710.20 U
8/9	1,740.00 U
8/10	1,781.30 U
8/18	1,818;90 U
8/19	1,848.90 U
8/22	1,888.70 U

Even the greenest investor in the world must appreciate the power of this phenomenal run. It was epic. Seven sips to get past 1,500, four swallows to pass by 1,600 and just three gulps apiece to navigate the 1,700 and 1,800's. But as gold continued to smash new 52 week high records at an ever faster pace there were some warning bells clanging around in the back of my brain.

First, I always keep two sets of numbers in my memory banks for every investment I follow. It is a very simple picture, a rough approximation of the trading range or where the support and resistance levels are. Without these two numbers, I am lost. If we are near the top of the trading range, I'm thinking about selling and if we are near support, I'm thinking about buying. The problem for me with gold was I could never get any handle on the support levels because there wasn't any meaningful sell off to establish the lower band of the risk-reward ratio. Gold would reach a new 52 week high and then lose a pittance of somewhere between fifty and a hundred bucks making the support level unidentifiable. The second clanging bell was gold's gap openings. A gap opening happens when there is a huge im balance between buyers and sellers before the opening bell. If there are more buyers than sellers, the opening is higher. If there are more sellers than buyers, the opening is lower. On August 8th, there was a significant gap opening for gold and it closed up a monster $61.40 for the day. Gap openings are a clear signal that the markets are trading on super heated emotions, that greed has overwhelmed any thoughts of risk.

Any time, you think there isn't any risk in a market, bend over because you are going to get a richly deserved spanking.

As gold began to trade near $1,900 an ounce there was a consensus thinking arms race on Wall Street to see who could predict how far above $2,000 an ounce could go. It was a pathetic orgy of crazy talk. It was a war of words, "$2,400 by February 2012: and "$3,000 by the end of 2012." There wasn't a single voice of concern that gold might meet massive resistance at $2,000 an ounce. When the Wall Street media lemmings are all stampeding in the same direction, you better think twice about joining the herd. There is some profound wisdom in having a contrarian point of view. It takes a lot of courage to think for yourself and maybe that's why the contras do so well? It doesn't matter what kind of investment you are talking about, fuzzy trading ranges, gap openings and Wall Street group think are all signals of a clear and present danger.

The fourth danger signal is by far the hardest to quantify, always expect the unexpected. The wild card or the joker in the deck. Whatever you think is an impossibility is usually more probable than you believe to be possible. On August 11th, the impossible happened when the CME raised Comex gold margin rates by 22%. On that day gold fell nearly 2% as investors fled the scene. But gold investors ignored this warning and continued to push gold higher and higher until it reached an inter day high of $1,917. 90 an ounce. As gold continued to heat up, no one brought up the fact that the CME raised silver margin rates back in May to prevent silver from blasting pass $50 an ounce. The buzz kill for silver clearly worked as silver immediately fell from a high of $48 to $30 over night. Silver has barely seen $40 an ounce ever since. When it was apparent that the powers to be were dead set against $2000 an ounce gold and speculators continued to bid its price up they decided to teach the market a very expensive lesson. They reacted by increasing the margin rate again on August 23rd, 2011. Gold prices behaved in an extremely violent manner and fell by more than $100 an ounce, the biggest one day drop since 1980. Investors continued dumping gold at a feverish pace until it bottomed out somewhere near $1,600 an ounce. One thing for sure, any investor who bought any gold in August 2011 needed an extra cap full of bleach to wash out their under shorts! As gold continued its free fall there were early signs of stress in the system as a small number of gold mining stocks began to make new 52 lows. These new lows were the first to appear in the system for any long position gold investments in quite awhile.

Interestingly, the experts pointed to two main reasons for gold's big sell off. One, an increasing US dollar versus the Euro as the sovereign debt crisis in the PIGS began to heat up. Second, they pinned the blame on investors being forced to pay for margin calls in other parts of their portfolios as the markets were starting to stagger under a constant stream of bad news. Virtually none of the on air experts ever brought up the root cause, the CME's vendetta against $2,000 an ounce gold. I wonder why?

As gold prices began to fall, gold mining stocks in the system started to wobble. Almost immediately, shares of Hecla (HL), Freeport Mc Moran (FCX) and Rio Tinto (RIO) hit new 52 week lows. I was kind of surprised by this because these stocks are in no way "weak sisters" that usually lead the pack down. By October 3rd,2011 the modern gold trading system was under an extreme amount of stress. It was a sort of future glimpse of hell in the system and its picture is invaluable as a supreme learning moment. Of all the case histories, this may be the most important.

Case History # 11: Gold, A System Under Stress

October 4,2011

For gold and silver, the new 52 week high switch for the futures has been in the OFF position as they seek to find support in a falling market. The gold futures contract is down $41.30 to close at $1,614.70. Silver is off nearly a buck, down 95 cents to close at $29.97. The pervasive emotion is pessimism in all the markets as the world rethinks the potential of a second world wide recession. The Universe of New 52 Week Highs

ZERO!

The Universe of New 52 Week Lows
The PHLX Gold/Silver Index was down by $4.19 to close at 178.79, a new low. On the NYSE, five stocks are making new lows. They were: Anglo Ashanti Gold ADS (AU 38.97), Anglo Ashanti Gold ADS Pfd A (AUPrA 46.82), Freeport Mc Moran (FCX 28.85), Kinross Gold (KGC 12.80) and US Gold Corp (UXG 3.32). The NYSE Amex chips in with ten gold and silver stocks making new lows. The losers were: Avino Gold (AVL 1.56), Brigus Gold (BRD .98), Entree Gold (EGI 1.15), Extorre Gold (XG 5.24), Gold Resources (GORO 15.06), Great Panther Silver (GPL 1.99), Lake Shore Gold (LSG 1.23), Minico Gold (MGH .71), Nova

Gold (NG 5.93), and Seabridge Gold (SA 19.84). On the NASDAQ, Pwr Shs Glbl Prec Metals (PSAU 38.73) joins the list of losers.

The NYSE Arca yields five new 52 week lows, all gold mining ETFs. They were: Glbl X Gold Explorers (GLDX 10.16), Clbl X Pure Gold Miners (GGGG 12.39), Market Vector Gold (GDX 50.42), Mkt Vector Junior Gold (JGDX 28.22) and DXNDLYGLDMNR2XBULL (NUGT 24.19). The total population of new 52 week lows for the modern gold trading universe was 21. This list will grow as gold and silver seek a new level of support.

Summary

There is so much educational meat here that I hardly know where to start carving the prime rib. Right off, the composition of the new 52 week lows in the modern gold trading system sticks out like a vegetarian at a fancy steak house. 100% of the new 52 week lows come exclusively from the gold mining sector of the system. Gold mining stocks had lagged behind bullion backed ETF's since way back in May and the crash in gold prices just pushed them farther apart. The fact that the PHLX Gold/ Silver Index , entirely composed of gold mining stocks, is hitting a new 52 week low and showing double digit losses for the year shows just how far away the bullion backed ETF's are. The bullion backed ETF's are still clinging to small gains for the year. The complete absence of bullion backed ETF's from the new 52 week lows list speaks volumes about where a conservative investor might want to place their bets.

The appearance of "cheap" third tier weak sister gold mining stock's on the new 52 week low list is a priceless lesson in investing. Really, really cheap stocks, those selling for a couple of bucks or less are traps or snares for investors. Because they sell for a low price, investor's tend to aggressively over buy them. It's really pretty easy to talk someone into buying a couple thousands shares of an el cheapo than a higher price, higher quality opportunity. Just because you bought something for a buck doesn't mean it was a bargain. When things fall apart, these cheap dogs will be the first to howl. When you hear them barking, it might be a good time to exit the system?

There are four lessons to store in your mental locker for future reference. Investments that go up and up without a sell off are very dangerous. You can count on it, the higher they go the bigger the fall. Gap openings are always trying to tell you something important. Emotion has gained to upper hand over rationality. Whenever that happens, big swings in the markets are on the horizon. While I ignore Wall Street experts advice, I always listen to what they say. When expert after expert say the same thing I grow apprehensive. The Old School experts are a herd of lemmings who are victims of group think. When they all start moving in the same direction, the opposite track begins to look very attractive Finally, you just have to be aware of the world you live in, No one, not a single soul should have been caught by surprise when margin rates got raised not only once but twice. They did it with great effect earlier to silver and when the first gold margin rate got bumped up and gold continued to go up, how could any one get caught off guard when they did it again? Sometimes, all the clues to the puzzle are there right in front of you. In the investment game, no one is going to put them together for you. It's really all on you.

At the very beginning of the modern gold trading system I said new parts were constantly being added to the system. There are some recent additions to the system, that in my opinion, will be game changers. They will be the very first indicators of trouble in the system. A kind of early warning system like the old NORAD. A big plus is they are also very easy to read. Some day, when to gold outhouse stuff really hits the fan they will prove to be invaluable. The new parts are like an 800 pound canary in the gold mine, a signal of impeding danger. They are Velocity Shares 3X Inverse Gold ETN (DGLD) and Velocity Shares 3X Inverse Silver ETN (DSLV). The immense amount of leverage means these will be the very first parts of the ETF side of the system to make new 52 week lows when gold starts in decline. I am thinking about ditching seven gold and silver stocks and ETF's for just three. They are DUST, DGLD, and DSLV. How can you read a system of more than 200 different parts by using just four parts? The first is and always will be the most important, the gold futures contracts. Where they go DUST, DGLD, and DSLV will not only follow, but will lead the pack. By watching the short side. I know what the long side is doing. If DUST,DGLD, and DSLV are making new 52 week lows, gold is going down. If they are away from making new highs, the gold market is in a state of transition. When gold behavior turns negative, they will be the very first to flash new 52 week high signals. I am not in the business of telling people what to buy or sell anymore. That dream died a very long time ago. My mission is to teach investors to think for themselves and when DUST, DGLD and DSLV all turn negative it means there's a new pricing cycle starting. The only fly in the ointment is these parts are so low they haven't gathered much in the way of volume. But as the machines learn how to use them to their advantage, volume will grow.

On December 13th,2011, gold futures shed an impressive $75.60 per contract and the modern gold trading system behaved true to form. Gold mining stocks, the PHLX Gold/Silver Index and gold mining stocks all experienced losses. The NYSE Amex suffered the most with 8 gold mining stocks making new 52 week lows. For the very first time, there was some really important action in the bullion driven ETF part of the system. Seven members of the ETF gold fraternity hit new 52 week lows. Most notable was DXNDLY GOLD MINER 3X BULL (NUGT), and Market Vector Jr. Gold (GDXJ). No surprises there. But, in a major shift, the were four bullion backed ETF's making new 52 week lows: Pro Shs Ult Silver (AGQ), VS 2X Platinum (UPLT), VS 3X Gold (UGLD), and VS 3X Silver (USLV). In ARCA land, there was one single, solitary new 52 week high, VS 3X Inverse Gold (DGLD). I am usually never a kind of " I told you so" kind of guy, but this may be the start of something very, very big. The massively leveraged (300%), Velocity Shares, long and short are moving in the opposite directions. Should you bail on bullion? I don't think so. The aggressive speculator may want to dump long ETF's at the top of the trading range ($1,750) and start to nibble away at the 3X inverse ETF. This may be very attractive to traders and a slow but cautious approach for long term investors.

I feel so blessed to see the sell off in gold. One, it gave me a glimpse of the future which is priceless. When you know what going to happen before it happens, you have all the marbles on your side.

Second, I finally got a very clear picture of the trading range. I work in round numbers, so I see it as support at $1.600 an ounce and resistance at $1,900. It seems lately that gold is meeting some near term resistance at $1,800. My very last look at gold prices for the book shows that on November 18th, 2011, gold lost $54.00 an ounce to close at $1,719. 90. It's just a guess, but I think gold will make a lower level past its support level long before resistance gets threatened? I think when the gold crash happens it will be in big chunks rather than small pieces. Gold will fall to new lows in a matter of weeks rather than months. The investor with vision who is prepared for action in advance will make just as much on gold's fall as they did on its rise. And that my friends is revolutionary

The Carnage in Gold Mining Stocks: 2012

This is the narrative of two completely different views of the same event: the carnage in gold mining stocks in 2012. Only one side will be right. It is up to you to judge the facts and make your own call.

The Old School Speaks

As 2011 was winding down, Old School stock pickers were solidly bullish about the future of gold mining stocks. The primary fuel for all the optimism was the belief that gold bullion would be trading north of $2,000 an ounce by March, 2012. Another cause for all hype, excuse me, hope was the prospect of another round of quantitative easing by the Fed, QE 3.

Here is a sampling of the general opinions of the experts at the time. First up to bat is Jon Markham in his op ed piece, "It's Time to Buy Gold Mining Stocks," published on October 14,2011. Markham is remarkably blunt in his opening statement, "If you're not investing in gold mining stocks, you should be." Markham presents five reasons to support his claim. They were: (1) gold mining stocks are cyclical and we are near the bottom of the buying range. (2) gold mining stocks are under pressure from rising input prices and lower oil prices should help the bottom line. (3) "...the stocks are cheap. Some are trading below ten times earnings...so if gold does indeed shoot over $2,000 in the next few months, as some have predicted, it's fair to expect margin expansion and gold earnings growth in a no growth world." (4) gold mining stocks are universally under owned. (5) "gold prices rose roughly $500 an ounce during QE 2. How far will it go if the Fed goes for QE 3 at some point?"

Markham is not the poster boy for bad behavior or fuzzy thinking among gold stock mining pimps. He is neither fish or fowl, but the norm. He is representative of all his contemporaries when it comes to gold mining stocks. I would read hundreds of reports and they all sounded like him.

Seven months later, on May 13, 2012, Old School advisers were still hawking gold mining stocks with an intense heat and a lot of passion. Next up to bat is "DF" from the firm, Wealth Engineering in near by Scottsdale. In the Sunday edition of the "Arizona Republic," there's a small section called "What They're Buying" where three financial advisers dispense with their best investment ideas. Here's "DF's" pitch. " Expects to see more stock market uncertainty, driven by developments in Europe. But he views that as a potential buying opportunity" for gold mining ETFs.

"DF" espouses global diversification and suggests having some gold assets as a hedge. He likes such funds as Vanguard Dividend Appreciation (VIG) and First Eagle Overseas (SGOIX), along with Market Vectors Gold Miners (GDX) which invests in gold mining stocks."

"DF" isn't an evil person. From the start of the year, there have been many financial advisers in the same section of the paper giving exactly the same advice. Buying gold mining stock ETF's seems to be the rage among financial consultants in 2012.

So what do we have? Pure gold financial advice or just a lump of fool's gold? What will be the truth about gold mining stocks in 2012?

The Modern Gold Trading System Speaks

The first hint of trouble in the modern gold trading system was just a gentle breeze of trouble. A zephyr so soft that it barely moved the curtains of an open window on a summer morning. On July 29, 2011, the gold futures were trending ever higher. With gold up $14.40, the futures closed at a new 52 week high of $1,628.30. There was dissent in the system as the PHLX Gold/Silver Index lost $ 4.83 for the day or a loss of negative 2.06%. Six gold bullion ETF's (AGOL, SGOL,IAU,DGP, DGL and UGL) all traded to new 52 week highs. My commentary reads, " There's a big disconnect between gold mining stocks and gold bullion ETFs. You better be careful!" One part of the system is headed north and another part is headed south.

Two months later, the winds of trouble are picking up. We are now facing a head wind of 40 knots It's time to batten down the hatches, put the patio furniture in the garage, and get ready. On October 4, 2011 the gold futures are down by $41.30 to close at $1614.70. **The PHLX Gold/Silver Index trades down to 178.79, a new 52 week low. The Index sheds $44.19 or 11.9% for the day. Year to date, the Index is down 21.1%!**

The entire system is pregnant with new 52 week lows, all of them, gold mining stocks and ETFs. It is an orgy of new 52 week lows. There are twenty new 52 week lows with the largest number in the NYSE Amex. GDX, GDXJ, GGGG and GLDX are all down by the bow and sinking fast. There isn't a new 52 week high to be found anywhere in the entire system.

By any Old School metrics, The PHLX Gold/Silver Index is now in Kodiak **BEAR** territory. There isn't a single reference to this extremely important development to be found anywhere by anyone. The Old School seems clueless to the dangers ahead.

The winds have kicked up to 60 knots and we are facing a tropical depression. Tons of rain and moderate property damage. On December 13,2011, the gold futures shed a massive $75.60 an ounce to close at $1,564.60. The PHLX Gold/Silver Index lose $5.24 for the day to close at 182.58, off 2.79% for the day. There are 23 new 52 week lows in the system. Two are highly leveraged gold bullion funds (UGLD and USLV). At 300% leverage, they are the canaries in the coal mine. The damage in the gold mining sector are significant. The only new 52 week high is DGLD, a highly leveraged (300%) gold bullion fund, which is up an impressive 10.8%!

During the last trading week of the year, we have a hurricane of massive proportions on our doorstep. I have titled the day's recap as, "We have Ignition: It's Time to Sell." Gold futures have plummeted by $23.10 to close at $1,539.90 and ounce. The new support level for bullion seems to be around the $1,525 mark. The PHLX Gold/Silver Index closes at 179.43, down for the year by 20.8%!

There are zero new 52 week highs on the NYSE. New 52 week lows include AuprA,IAG, and KGC. There are zero new 52 week highs on the NYSE Amex. New 52 weeks lows are BRD and SA. There are zero new 52 week highs on the NASDAQ. The Lone Ranger new 52 week low is PSAU. There is one new 52 week high on the NYSE Arca: DGLD. New 52 week lows for the NYSE Arca include: NUGT,GLDX, GGGG, GDX, GDXJ, and UGLD.

You don't need a PhD to see what's going on. If you had any doubt, the main stays of the Old School pimps, GDX and GDXJ, are on fire, "sells" with multiple new 52 week lows. The PHLX Gold/Silver Index is in bear territory with a year to date loss of negative 20.8 %! The bear signal of a loss of twenty percent is one of the sacred cows of the Old School. They either don't know or care? Either way, it spells big problems for the investors who are turning to them for advice. **As 2011 winds down, we have two directly opposite views of the same subject. The Old School is bullish on all things gold mining stocks. However, the modern gold trading system is screaming that all things gold mining stocks is definitely a SELL! Only one can be right and which one will prevail in 2012?**

The Moment of Truth: 2012

My opening is dedicated to every E-4 who served their country in any branch of the military. What happened to the gold mining sector in the first five months of 2012 was FUBAR (Fouled Up Beyond Recognition) and SNAFU (Situation Normal All Fouled Up) at the same time. It was a cluster foul up of gargantuan proportions. In its violence and intensity, it looked remarkably similar to the market meltdown of 2008. This behavior will give us a clue to what really happened.

By March 2012, it was abundantly clear that gold bullion was not going to smash the $2,000 an ounce barrier. The idea of Q-3 was nothing more than a mirage. I have mixed feelings about all the hype that surrounds $2,000 an ounce gold. First, it hasn't happened in 5,000 years of history. Why any conservative investor would place a bet on something that has never happened bugs me? $2,000 an ounce gold may very well be a hollow victory. I think there's going to be an extraordinary number of sellers world wide who are going to dump gold the nanosecond it hits $2,000 an ounce. Every time it balloons to two grand an ounce, sellers are going to come out of the wood work. I won't feel comfortable with two g's for gold until that level becomes a support level opposed to being a major resistance level. This will take time. As far as 2012 goes, gold bullion for the first five months will lag against the Dow but perform better than bonds.

I was looking forward to adjusting my universe with the addition of the highly leveraged DIREXIONDAILYGOLDMINER'S, NUGT (long) and DUST (short). For those who are new to the game, the DIREXIONDAILYGOLD-MINER'S, are the Market Vectors Gold Miners ETF (GDX) on steroids and human growth hormones. The only thing I don't like about them is the income components. Who are we trying to fool? An income kicker with a highly leveraged investment does not make them any less dangerous! As far as the gold mining segment of the universe goes, DUST is the ONLY short side of the game available.

While the problems for the gold mining shares initially started in 2011, my first thought was we were experiencing a natural bout of profit taking. If you looked through the long lens of time, the gold mining shares had appreciated along ways. I would change that opinion with the first five months of 2012. Between January 3 and March 12,2012, gold mining shares would decline seven out of ten weeks. In a couple of those weeks, losses were ten per cent or more. Old School pundits of profit would fall all over themselves to try and come up with reasons for the decline. They would set blog land afire blaming the losses on increased entry costs (energy and labor), increased royalty fees, and poor management decisions. I wasn't buying any of it! At first, I thought Old School stock pickers were re-evaluating gold mining shares based on declining bullion prices. Stupid me. When I reviewed the literature, they were still hooked on $2,000 an ounce bullion. Besides, they would never have the mental dexterity or moxie to make such a call. Starting with the week of March 19, 2012, the reason for the decline in gold mining shares was clear. We were seeing an attack by short sellers using computers to manipulate the gold mining shares segment of the system.

The Dark Side of the Moon: Short Selling

For the average American investor, the act of short selling is like the dark side of the moon. Both are distant, mysterious and a little sinister. The truth is, it would be more likely for an investor to visit the dark side of the moon than to ever do a short sale. I know the investment lingo by heart. An investor who believes the shares of XYZ Corporation are going to fall and wants to make a profit. They borrow shares of XYZ from a broker at $100 a share. After XYZ falls to $90 a share, the investor buys XYZ in the open market and replaces the borrowed shares for a $10 a share profit. I am 67 years old and have been intimately involved with stocks since 1975 (37 years) and I've never done a short sale and I have never seen one done. If my life depended on successfully completing a short sale, I'd be toast.

Almost since the beginning of US history there have been attempts to ban short selling. In fact, short selling was banned in America from the end of the 1812 War to the mid 1850's. Apparently, the young banking system and the infant stock market were too fragile to withstand the shocks of short selling. In the 1850's, the battle between the Bulls (long) and the Bears (short) somehow changed into a morality play of Good (long) versus Evil (short). The reason that short sellers were cast as evil doers was they used rumors to drive the price of a stock down. This complaint will resonate against short sellers through out investment history. According to the Bulls, short sellers and rumor mongering were the the causes of the Panic of 1907, the Crash of 1929, the Great Depression of the 1930's, the fall of Enron in 2001 and the Crash of 2008. If I knew it was so easy to blame short sellers for everything bad, I would have blamed them for my 15 units of "F" from Long Beach City College in 1964, my DUI in 1967 and my two failed marriages. Blaming the Great Depression on short sellers is like claiming root beer is the cause of alcoholism! Crazy, short sided and just plain wrong.

The charge that short sellers are evil because they spread rumors is a big fat red herring. When it comes to spreading rumors and the stock market, what is good for the gander apparently isn't so good for the goose. The Bulls have been using rumors to hype stock prices since the get go! Today, they even have an investment maxim to explain the bull. It is, buy the rumor and sell the fact. I can't count the times I've heard a broker say something like " I got some hot dope off the grapevine," "my sources tell me," and "according to the rumor mill." I'd say, that when it comes to manipulating stock prices using rumors, the Bulls and the Bears are just about dead even. A tie between liars and cheats.

The hate against short sellers on Wall Street runs as deep as the Mariana's Trench in the Pacific Ocean. It borders on a pathological rage that is irrational. Consider what Richard Fuld, CEO of Lehman Brothers had to say about short sellers. " When I find a short seller, I want to tear his heart out and eat it before his eyes while he's still alive." All this anger and hate has given me the idea for an original joke. A young man is about to confront his father who is a steadfast Republican and heads an investment banking firm. " Dad, I have to confess that I am a Democrat." "That's okay son, we can live with that." " Dad, I am gay." "That's okay son, we can live with that." "Dad, I am a short seller." "Get out of the house, you rotten SOB!"

Why all the animosity directed at short sellers? The answer is extremely important to your investment future. They hate short sellers because they upset the natural order of things in the universe of the Bulls. For the Bulls, there is one thing that is codified and cast in stone. To make money, you buy low, hold and sell high. Anything else is heresy. Short sellers who buy high and sell low are the fly in the sugar. The Bulls will go to any lengths to discredit them. In the early 1990's, Ray Dirks, a controversial figure on Wall Street started something called The Short Busters Club. Dirks would solicit money to buy into short positions making the stocks go up. It wasn't about buying a stock for its investment value but a chance to punish the shorts. If this doesn't qualify as gross manipulation, what does?

In 2008, the Bullish cry babies were at it again by claiming short sellers were spreading rumors about banking stocks and driving them into the toilet. The unfunny thing is the rumors proved to be true, particularly those, concerning

Bear Stearns. The SEC would ban short selling in nearly 800 stocks for a short period of time to stem the plummeting market. I don't get it. Why punish the shorts for being right?

What kind of protection does the average "little guy" have against short sellers? Today, the answer is simple .**Nothing! Zero! Zip! Nada! Zilch!** They are as defenseless as a two year old, naked infant, against a hungry lion. This wasn't always the case. For nearly 70 years, individual investors, were protected by the Up Tick Rule. The Securities Act of 1934, beautifully crafted by Joseph P. Kennedy, began to set the rules for short sellers. After a market crash in 1937, the SEC instituted the Up Tick Rule in 1938.In general, it said that an institution could only short a stock that was going up. The rule was meant to act as a set of brakes to slow the momentum of stock prices careening downhill.

What the SEC gives, the SEC takes away. In 2007, in a stunning move, the SEC did away with the uptick rule on July 6th. **It is not a mere coincidence that one year later, the stock market crashed to 1930's levels.** The removal of the uptick rule did not cause the 2008 market crash, it just made it worse. Without the protection of the uptick rule, individual investors would be financially crucified to the benefit of Black Box short sellers.

There would be efforts to restore the uptick rule. Muriel Siebert, a pioneer on Wall Street said, "we're watching history being made. The SEC took away the short sale rule when the markets were falling, institutional investors just pounded stocks because they didn't need an uptick." On March 28,2008, Jim Cramer claimed that the absence of the uptick rule harms stock markets. I wish that Cramer would have sent his followers into the streets as a show of public protest. It's the only thing that the politicos in DC understand.

It is truly ironic that the one institution charged with the protection of small, individual investors, the SEC, has been the leader in destroying any and all of the rules that were designed to protect them. The sad, sad truth is the SEC is really a paid lobbyist for the interests of Wall Street. They have been the lead dog in the dismantling of the Securities Exchange Act of 1934, the only laws on the books, that had the best interests of the individual investor in mind!

The Great Bear Market Raid Against Gold Mining Stocks (2012)

In the 19th century, when short sellers banded together to drive the price of a stock down, it was called a bear market raid. In 2012, Black Box operators orchestrated a massive and complex bear market raid against the gold mining stocks, gold mining indexes, and gold mining ETF's. They wouldn't use rumors to drive prices down. Rumors? We don't need no stinking rumors! All we need is a computer algorithm.

The great gold mining raid would have three distinct parts: the skirmishing, the assault, and the capitulation. The skirmishing began in 2011 and lasted until March 2012. There were terrible casualties in the gold mining stock sector as they began to sink to new 52 week lows. That directly caused new 52 week lows in the gold stock indexes and gold mining ETFs. Those multiple new lows (two) will translate to universal sell signals. During the first ten weeks of the new year, the modern gold trading system will lose money seven out of ten weeks. What caught my eye was that parts of the system were shedding ten per cent a week in value.

The assault phase of the bear raid began in March 2012 and it was violent and vicious. We will look at the murderous declines of GDX and NUGT during the bear raid. The Black Box operators were short the gold mining stocks and stock indexes. To guarantee they would decline, all they had to do was sell the gold mining ETF's. In other systems, they short the stocks, indexes, the futures and sell the ETFs. It's like shooting halibut in a barrel.

The Fall of GDX

There are five major gold mining ETF's: GDX, GGGG, RING, PSAU and NUGT. Of the five, the most widely followed and popular is GDX. Starting for the week of March 17th to May 19th, GDX would make eight new 52 week lows. **None of the experts would take note.** For them, they are clueless or 52 week lows are not a metric for fundamental or technical analysts?

The dates and new 52 week lows for GDX were: March 17th-48.42D, March 24th-48.05D, March 31st-46.00D, April 7th-45.98D, April 21st-44.18D April 28th-43.40D, May 12th-41.08D, and May 19th-39.08D.Since its sell signal close of 51.43 on December 27, 2011, GDX will plummet $12.35 a share or a stunning 24%! The small, retail customer will never know what hit them and their financial advisers won't have an explanation. It was a bear market raid by computers.

Two Days of Hell: April 9-10,2012

Even as gold bullion prices were on the up draft, gold mining shares and ETFs were in the negative doldrums. On April 9th, 2012, the Dow was down by 130.55 points, gold futures were up by $14.00 to close at 16452.50 an ounce and the

PHLX Gold/Silver Index traded to a new 52 week low of 165.30D. In the system there were eight new 52 week lows, most notably in the NYSE Arca, the gold mining ETFs: Global X Gold Explorer (GLDX) at 9.15D, Global X Gold Miners (GGGG) at 11.28D, and Market Vectors Junior Gold Miners (GDXJ) at 22.24D.

April 10th was even worse as the world worries about the PIGS. In one of the worst trading days of the year, the Dow lost 213.66 points. However, gold futures were strong winners for a second day in a row. Gold futures gained $17.00 to close at 1659.50.

Unfortunately, the gold mining sector suffered dramatic losses as the PHLX gold/Silver Index traded down again to another new 52 week low of 164.07D. The NYSE kicked in with six losers making new 52 week lows: Anglo Gold Ashanti (AU) 32.44D, Anglo Gold Ashanti PrA (AUPrA) 39.51D, El Dorado Gold (EGO) 12.44D, Gold Fields ADS (GFI) 12.53D, Harmony Gold (HMY) 9.90D, and Hecla Mines (HL) 4.09D.

It was an ugly scene in the NYSE Arca complex if you were long. It was a beautiful masterpiece if you were short. The five new 52 week lows were: Global X Gold Explorers (GLDX) 9.04D, Global X Gold Miners (GGGG) 11.14D, iSH MSCI Global Silver (SLVP) 21.37D, Market Vector Gold (GDX) 45.98 and Junior Market Vector Gold (GDXJ) 22.01D.

There were two new 52 week lows on the NYSE Amex. On the NASDAQ, Pwr Shs Global Gold&Precious Metals (PSAU) 36.36D was the big loser of the day.

Something sucks! All gold mining stocks and ETFs are downers and all gold bullion ETFs are winners. When you look at the gold mining system it is rotten to the core as the gold mining stocks and the gold mining stock ETFs are totally simpatico in their slide. That is, because they are really one in the same.

The Fall of NUGT

The first thing I have to say about NUGT is it isn't an early warning system or the 800 pound canary in the coal mine. GDX and NUGT are congruent with one another and nearly trade in tandem. The only difference is NUGT will make or lose money three times faster than GDX.

Here are the dates and new 52 week lows for NUGT: March 17th-16.58D, March 24th-15.85D, March 31st-14.93D, April 7th-12.91D, April 28th-11.35D, May 5th-10.65D, May 12th-9.02D, and May 19th-7.69D. In the case of NUGT, the money wasn't lost but transferred to another ETF.

From its January 3rd close of 21.61, NUGT will drop a stunning 13.92 a share or a crushing 65%!

The Modern Gold Trading System Speaks Again

The modern gold trading system will speak one more time during the bear market raid against gold mining stocks. All systems have a very small vocabulary: buy and sell. The system will issue two sell signals (GDX,NUGT) and one buy signal (DUST). The two sell signals represented a massive number of sell signals representative of the entire system at large. During the entire raid, there was only one buy signal, DUST.

The Sell Signals

ETF	Date	
GDX	3/17	3/24
High	50.52	50.95
Low	48.42D	48.05D
Close	49.76	49.54 **SELL**
NUGT	3/17	3/24
High	20.56	17.46
Low	16.58D	15.55D
Close	16.88	16.62 **SELL**

The Buy Signal

ETF	Date	
DUST	4/28	5/5
High	56.56U	58.50U
Low	46.67	47.24
Close	47.65	56.65 **BUY**

The entire gold mining system was screaming "sell me" save one part, DUST, who was shouting "buy me." The buy signal came late in the game which was a minor disappointment. It was just a function of the numbers. DUST would gain huge chunks of value weekly but would just miss new 52 week highs by a small amount. I don't think there is a human on the planet that could have traded DUST for such a short period of time. The best advice the system was spreading was switch to cash!

The Rise of DUST

In the entire gold mining system, there was just one winner in the universe. It was a super nova performer, the Direxion 3x Inverse Gold Mining Stocks, DUST. After all the dust settled, some bozo wrote a piece called " The Best Investment No One Ever Heard Of " detailing the performance of DUST. We will detail the rise of DUST in three segments: the build up, the new 52 week highs and the buying orgy in the last week of climbing prices.

The build up phase lasted fifteen weeks, starting for the week of January7th and ending April 21st. The closing numbers and the gains and losses for the week were January 7th and a closing price of 37.70 per share. The next weeks close was 36.15 (1.55), 39.88 +3.73, 29.44 (10.44), 30.16 +.72, 33.46 +3.36, 33.84 +.38, 29.57 (4.27), 31.94 +2.37, 34.47 +2.53, 41.55 +7.08, 41.73 +.18, 41.97 +.24, 50.74 +8.87, 46.17 (4.57, and 50.25 +4.08. For the fifteen week build up phase there are eleven winners for a winning batting average of 73%! The gain is a plus 12.25 per share for a gain of 33%! You ain't seen nothing yet.

The next phase of new 52week highs will last four weeks, starting on April 28th and ending on the week of May 19th. The new 52 week highs were: 56.53U, 58.70U, 68.74U and 78.66U. From its starting point close of 37.70 for the week of January 7th to the week of May 19th, DUST will gain a gargantuan 40.96 per share. **This is a monster gain of 109% in five months!**

An Orgy of Buying: The Week of May 18th, 2012.

Date	Open	High	Close	Volume
May 14	63.15	68.92U	68.85	347,400
May 15	67.11	72.46U	77.02	319,000
May 16	69.25	78.66U	76.04	461,300
May 17	62.00	72.48	65.66	392,000
May 16	65.01	58.66	64.30	313,100

What an incredible week of volatility. From its high of 78.66 to its low of 58. 66, DUST will lose 20.00 a share for a loss of 25%! From its open of 63.15 to its all time new 52 week high of 78.66 just three days later, DUST will gain 15.51 a share. This is, you guessed it, a gain of 25%! You would need a cast iron gut and a pretty incredible ticker to stand the stress. Even better yet, if you were a computer, it was all just a game of numbers.

In general, I always measure moves from close to close. In this case, I measured from the close to the all time market high for a very specific reason. I don't believe for a second that any humans could have bought at the close in January and clocked the profits at the all time high of $78.66 a share and that's the point. The truth is that only a computer could book those profits and they did. High frequency traders executed billions of millisecond trades to lock in a penny a share profit all the way from 37.70 to 78.66. This was not a human experience! The big question is: why didn't humans participate in one of the all time great money making opportunities? This is one of those "light bulb" moments. I am so anxious for you to see the truth. You never heard about this chance of a life time because for your financial adviser, it just didn't exists. For them, it would be "un-American" or "like rooting against the home team." They hate the short side so much that they will never, ever, guide you to the short side, no matter how profitable it might be! **This makes your financial adviser a one trick pony!** They are bound to the buy low, hold and sell high model and nothing will ever convince them to do other wise.

In my universe in 2012, there were significantly more buy signals than sell signals. The big winners in the buy side of my universe are : T, AAPL, MSFT (a shock), HD, and WMT. While their gains have been respectable, the move in DUST, makes them look like 98 pound weaklings. In fact, I have collected data for 1,300 consecutive weeks and I can't remember a single instance where anything ever moved up more than 100% in just five months. Nothing even comes close. This is the power of machine driven investment strategies. There is a precedent to this kind of machine behavior and the year was 2008. Every-one has their own memories of 2008. Most remember that was the year that the big banks got bailed out. It is just my opinion, but I think it was a horrific idea. I wish we would have let AIG, Bank of America, Bear Stearns, Citigroup and Merrill Lynch go belly up. By subsidizing their bad behavior, we have just post phoned a bigger crisis in the future. There is a small number of Americans who are aware of the trillions of nearly "free" loans the banks got from the Fed. I can't find anyone who is aware the banks made **BILLIONS** of dollars in profits by trading inverse ETFs! No one asked the most obvious question: if you made billions in high frequency trading profits, why did you need a bail out?

The behavior of the computers in 2008 and the great bear raid of 2012 would have some remarkable similarities. Both lasted around seven months. This means these opportunities were a trade and not a long term investment. Can humans trade? There were extreme blow ups for the inverse ETFs. There were extreme sell offs in the long side ETFs. Both examples were marked by immense volumes at the close of the events.

I think a fair question about the great bear raid of 2012 would be: who did it? As in any crime, all you have to do, is consider who had the means, the motive, and the opportunity to create and execute such a strategy. I would probably start with the four unnamed firms accused of manipulating gold prices at the expiration of options. I wish I had the skills of an investigative reporter because there is a big story here. To find out, who done it, there are just a few questions that need to be answered. **Who was short gold mining stocks, gold mining indexes, and gold mining ETFs on March 17th to May 19th? Who was long PUTS for gold mining stocks, gold mining indexes, and gold mining ETFs on March 17th to May 19th? Here's the nail in the coffin for these high frequency traders. Who was long the Drixion Inverse 3X Gold Miners (DUST) on March 17th to May 19th? Who was long CALLS for DUST from March 17th to May 19th, 2012?** Good luck getting any straight answers from the government authorities.

It's a Small, Small, Small, Small World

The skeptics out there are probably saying, " it is just impossible to manipulate so many different parts of a massive trading system all at the same time." In actuality, the modern gold trading system is a tiny system with just a few parts.

Toward the end of this project, after identifying and matching all the parts, I was surprised just how small the modern gold trading system really is. All in all, only about seventeen gold mining stocks form two stock indexes and four ETFs. Out of that number, ten are super stars, appearing multiple times in different components. For those who want to doubt there is a system, consider the "ripple effect" of just one gold mining stock, Kinross Gold Corporation (KGC). ANY change in KGC will ripple through eight different system components. It is no coincidence that KGC will fall further than its comparable brothers and sisters in the system during the bear raid.

Stock	Symbol	Index and ETF Membership
Agnico-Eagle Mines	AEM	XAU,HUI
Anglo Gold Ashanti	AU	XAU,HUI,GDX,RING,PSAU, NUGT, DUST
Allied Nevada Gold Corporation	ANV	HUI,GGGG

Barrick Gold Corporation	ABX	XAU,HUI,GDX,RING,PSAU, NUGT, DUST
Compania Mina Buenaventura	BVN	XAU,HUI,GDX,RING
El Dorado Gold	ELD	HUI,GDX,PSAU,RING,GGG, NUGT, DUST
Freeport McMoran Copper&Gold	FCX	XAU
Gold Corporation	GG	XAU,HUI,GDX,RING,PSAU, NUGT, DUST
Gold Fields	GFI	XAU,HUI,GDX,RING,PSAU, NUGT, DUST
Harmony Gold Mining	HMY	XAU,HUI
IAMGOLD Corporation	IMG	HUI
Kinross Gold Corporation	KGC	XAU,HUI,GDX,RING, GGGG, PSAU, NUGT,DUST
Newmont Mining Corporation	NEM	XAU,HUI,GDX,RING, PSAU,NUGT, DUST
New Gold Inc.	NGD	HUI
Randgold Resources	GOLD	XAU,HUI,GGGG
Royal Gold	RGLD	XAU
Yamana Gold	AUY	XAU,HUI,GDX,RING, PSAU,NUGT, DUST

There is one final point to ponder. It is important to note that most of the members in the modern gold trading system are mid to small capitalization stocks. Without a hundred dollar, big capitalization stock, this is a very cheap system to manipulate.

The Final Picture Show: May 17th, 2012

I am the world's worst photographer. I usually end up with red eyes and missing heads. The truth be known, I tossed the camera out a long time ago. It was pure luck (maybe) that my snapshot of the worst day (the bottom) of the bear market raid against the gold mining system was the best picture I ever took. It was a massive day of minus signals and a tremendous number of new 52 week lows. For me, the most exciting aspect of the day was the initial appearance of action in the gold bullion sector of the system. If you were short, the picture was exquisite. If you were long, the picture was grotesque. The same data with two different viewpoints.

The gold futures were down, testing new ten month lows. Both contracts were down by $20.50 with the 100 oz. And the mini-50 oz closing at 1,536.60.

The PHLX Gold/Silver Index (AUX) will close down to a new 52 week low. XAU opened at 146.46, hit a new 52 week low of 140.94D and close at 142.34. In round numbers, from its 52 week high of 228, XAU will shed 88 points for a stunning loss of 39% in less than a year!

There were ZERO new 52 week highs in the gold mining stock portion of the NYSE. There were nine new 52 week lows in gold mining shares on the NYSE. The losers were: Aurico Gold (AUQ) 6.69D, Barrick Gold (ABX) 24.82D, Gold Fields (GFI) 56.90D, Gold Corporation (GG) 32.16D, Harmony Gold (HMY) 11.71D, I am Gold (IAG) 9.20D, Newmont Gold (NEM) 43.23D and Seabridge Gold (SA) 12.20D. It is no coincidence that all the new 52 week lows on the NYSE are members of one or more gold mining ETFs.

There were ZERO new 52 week highs in the gold mining sector of the NYSE Amex. There were eight new 52 week lows. The downers were: Allied NV Gold (ANV) 23.69D, Avino Silver&Gold Mines 1.12D, Extorre Gold Mines (XG) 2.15D, Great Basin Gold (GBG) .48D, Minco Gold (MGH) .43D, New Gold (MGH) 7.13D, Timmins Gold (TGD) 1.55D and Seabridge Gold (SA) 12.20D.

There were ZERO new 52 week highs in the gold mining sector of the NAS-DAQ. There was one new 52 week low on the NASDAQ. The loser was Global Gold and Precious Metals Portfolio (PSAU) 30.55D.

For me, the most interesting action was found in the NYSE Arca. In the entire modern gold trading system there was just one single, solitary new 52 week high, DirexionDAILYGOLDMINER'S BEAR 3X Shares (DUST) at a mind blowing 78.66 a share. There were six new 52 week lows for the long ETFs. They were: DirectionDAILYGOLDMINER'S BULL 3x Shares (NUGT) 7.69D, 2X Gold Bull&S&P 500 Bear (FSG) 21.60D, Gold Explorers ETF (GLDX) 6.36D, Pure Gold Miners ETF (GGGG) 9.21D, Market Vectors Gold Miners (GDX)39.08D and Market Vectors Junior Gold Miners ETF (GDXJ) 17.37D.

For the first time, we have action in the bullion ETF sector and it would involve the long portion of the system. The new 52 week lows were: PowerShares DB Gold Double Long ETN (DGP) 44.22D, PowerShares DB Precious Metals Fund (DBP) 50.18D, and ProShares Ultra Gold (UGL)73.75D.

I am a praying man and I thank God that I got to see today with my own one good eye. This will be the absolute bottom of the bear market raid. For technicians, this is the exact bottom of a pivot point for the gold mining stocks (they won't know it). The very next day, the entire modern gold trading system will start to move up. The lone exception is DUST which will start to lose massive amounts of value.

The most exciting part of the day was the first signs of stress in the gold bullion sector of the system. The early new 52 week lows will be the extremely leveraged part of the system. Unlike NUGT and DUST, it looks like the highly leverage bullion ETFs **are** early warning systems and are like the 800 pound canary in the mine. One thing for sure, gold bullion near 1,536.60 will ignite the hyper leveraged ETFs. The only disappointment is the most leveraged of the gold bullion ETFs, UGLD and DGLD did not appear of the new 52 week high or low list. Maybe, they came within a penny and just missed by a whisker?

The Aftermath

When it was all over, I put everything away, so I could have a chance to digest everything that had happened. I wanted to have time to reflect so I didn't jump to any bogus conclusions. There were any number of casualties in the great bear market raid against gold mining stocks. The small, individual investor, would suffer on two fronts: their psyches and pocket books.

The number one problem for investors will be the erosion of confidence in the market. After the 2008 disaster, the Flash Crash shortly there after, investors with some justification felt the market was "rigged" against them. For investors, they will feel like they have been robbed of the "American dream" of building wealth by investing in stocks. Who can blame them?

The crash in gold mining stocks will send investors into a more dangerous trading system:bonds. The bond system is more highly leveraged, more sophisticated, and more "invisible" than any of the other trading systems. Most of its trades are hidden behind the veil of the OTC market. Investors will trust their wealth to the same old, tired strategy that burned them in stocks. They will buy low, hold and hope to sell high. They lost 40% of their net worth in 2008 by doing that and I predict even larger losses in the future for bonds!

One thing for sure, brokers ("DF") will shy away from gold mining ETFs for the future. It's a once burned, twice shy mentality. Brokers may stay away from ETFs forever? Who can blame them? Investors will think twice about buying ETFs as well. Who can blame them? Initially, I thought ETFs were built as an alternative to mutual funds. I liked them because they were cheap to buy, cheap to own, highly liquid, and diversified. I was completely wrong. ETFs were constructed to the advantage of computerized trading. **They are short term trading tools and NOT long term investments.**

The last damage to the psyche of investors will be a horrible consequence. Turned off by investing in stocks and ETFs, investors may fall into the arms of Ponzi schemers. After having been screwed in limited partnerships, in 1987, in the dot.com disaster, in Enron, in World Com, in Auction Rate Securities in 2008, in the Flash Crash and now the mess in gold mining stocks, the world of "safe" alternative investments looks mighty tempting. Who can blame them?

The damage to the pocket books of the small retail investor remains cloaked in secrecy. The reason for the losses are placed clearly on the shoulders of the investors and their advisers. After a decade of a secular bull market in gold bullion and gold mining stocks going along for the ride, they thought it was going to be "easy money" in 2012. With experts predicting $2,000 an ounce gold, how could they go wrong? Memo to everyone: there isn't anything that is "easy money" when it comes to investing. It's a perverse market where the unexpected is to be expected. Who would have dreamed that the computers would raise hell with gold mining shares? The computers did and they foretold the entire world of their intentions in 2011.

The Modern Gold Trading System: Redux

My view of the modern gold trading system has changed over time with the weight of added data and changing market conditions. The modern gold trading system isn't some Rube Goldberg contraption that was cobbled together by chance.

It is very much like all the other trading systems I have observed. The modern gold trading system is constructed like the oil, Major Market Index, the Dow 30, the S&P 100, the S&P 500 and the NASDAQ 100 Trust. They are all a combination of futures, indexes, stocks, ETFs, and options. They are intelligently designed with an architecture that transmits money at dazzlingly phenomenal speed between the different parts. They are the product of careful thought, exceptional efficiency, and a well organized structure.

The trading systems did not happen over night. They are based on an electronic evolutionary blue print that was decades in the making. They were clearly intended to enhance the position of algorithmic traders at the expense of traditional, retail investors. The entities could have only been the product of the collusion between New York bankers, Wall Street attorneys and Washington DC politicos. This is another of those light bulb moments that illustrates the cozy relationship between NY and DC. None of what happened in 2008 or the bear market raid on gold mining stocks in 2011-2012 without the uptick rule being canned by regulators. Without the change, inverse ETFs would have been held hostages by the uptick rule. This might surprise you, but I am glad they did away with the uptick rule. It opened a whole new world to retail investors. For the first time in history they could make triple digit returns on the short side without the hassle of a short sale. Only a crazy person would be angry with the Old School advisers for not getting out of gold mining stocks in 2011. They didn't know of its existence and they are not mind readers. On the other hand, you have to wonder about a group of experts who failed to notice the PHLX Gold/ Silvers Index was down by more than 20% by the end of 2011? You have to wonder why none of the experts were aware or concerned that GDX and GDXJ were making a series of new 52 week lows by the end of 2011? **The system was very clear in predicting big problems in the gold mining sector in 2011-2012 and it was right and all the experts were wrong!**

Maybe the biggest lesson to be learned has to do with the systems themselves? The days of buying any investment without regard to which system it belongs to and how that system is behaving is over. Null and void.

The modern gold trading system is an interconnected spider web of computers. There are two different systems. They are the gold mining sector and the gold bullion sector. They both feed on the price of gold, either directly (gold bullion) or indirectly (gold mining).

The Modern Gold Trading System: The Gold Mining Sector

The Ignition Points: (1) Old School metrics: PE's, dividends, capital structures, etc. etc. etc. (2) gold bullion prices and (3) algorithmic trading.

The NYSE: Anglo Gold Ashanti (AU), Agnico-Eagle Mines (AEM), Barrick Gold (ABX), Compania de Minas Buenaventura (BVN), El Dorado Gold (EGO), Freeport McMoran Copper&Gold (FCX), Gammon Gold (GRS), Gold Corp (GG), Gold Fields (GFI), Harmony Gold (HMY), IAMGOLD (IAG), Kinross Gold (KGC), Newmont Mining (NEM) and Yamana Gold (AUY).

Stock Indexes: PHLX Gold/Silver Index (XAU) and AMEX Gold Bug Index (HUI). **NYSE**

AMEX: Almaden Minerals(AAU), Fronteer Development Group (FRG), Keegan Resources (KGN), Nova Gold Res (NG) and Vista Gold Corp (VGZ). **NASDAQ:** Lahir Gold (LIHR), Randgold Resources (GOLD), and Royal Gold (RGLD).

NYSE ARCA: Market Vector Gold Miners (GDX), Market Vector Junior Gold Miners (GDXJ), iShares MSCI Global Miners (RING), Global X Gold Explorers (GLDX), Power Shares Global Gold&Precious Metals (PSAU), Global X Pure Gold Miners (GGGG) and Direxion Daily Gold Miner Bull 3X (NUGT). **Inverse Gold Mining ETF:** DirexionDailyGoldMiner Bear 3X (DUST). Additional Parts include open end mutual funds, closed end mutual funds, and options.

Jim Cramer is my new favorite comedian, boo yah! When he talks about "homework" and doing thirty minutes of research a week per stock position, I howl with laughter. While there are lots of parts to the modern gold trading system, in looking at the gold mining sector, to keep the whole shooting match under control, just follow XAU and/or GDX on a weekly basis. It will take less than 30 seconds to harvest the weekly high, low and close on Yahoo! Finance.

The Invisible Modern Gold Trading System: Gold Mining Stocks

In reality, there are two modern gold trading systems that co-exists every trading day. One, you can see quite clearly. You can find it everyday in your financial news source du jour: the Wall Street Journal, Investor's Business Daily, the "Business Section" of your local newspaper or Barron's on the week end. The second,the invisible computer system, is significantly larger and hidden from view. You would have to dig deep to find this one. Your financial advisor probably couldn't find it on their best day, let alone explain how it works. It consists of the same elements of the visible world: gold mining common stocks, indices, ETFs, and mutual funds. I believe the invisible world is used primarily by institutional investors/

It can be found on Yahoo! It is pretty simple. First, find the company you want, plug in its stock symbol in the quote box in the upper left hand corner. For example, if you are interested in Kinross Gold, type in KGC. Look to the far left, click on "components" under COMPANY a whole new electronic universe will be revealed.

Components of the Invisible Universe

Common Stocks of the Visible World	Symbol	Indices	ETFs	Mutual Funds
Agnico Eagle Mines	AEM	4	1	63
Anglo Gold Ashanti	AU	8	2	103
Allied Nevada Gold	ANV	0	0	3
Barrick Gold Mines	ABX	9	6	181
Compania Buenaventura	BVN	6	0	28
El Dorado Gold	ELO	4	3	43
Freeport McMoran	FCX	10	10	218
Gold Corp	GG	8	4	32
Gold Fields	GFI	6	4	27
Harmony Gold	HMY	6	0	3
I AM Gold	IMG	2	0	0
Kinross Gold	KGC	6	4	58
Newmont Mining	NEM	10	13	144
New Gold	NGD	3	0	0
Randgold Res	GOLD	30	1	85
Royal Gold	RGLD	49	1	19
Yamana Gold	AUY	4	1	56

The biggest single disparity between the visible and invisible computer worlds was found among the indexes. In the visible world there are two indexes and in the invisible world there were a stunning 165! Kinross Gold was a Saint Bernard in the visible cosmos and turned into a Poodle in the invisible world. Newmont Mining was a Chihuahua in the visible planet transformed itself into a Rottweiler in the invisible side. Freeport McMoran (FCX) and Barrick Gold went from shelter mutts to pure bred winners in the invisible side.

The huge surprise was the massive showing of Royal Gold (RGLD) and Randgold (GOLD) who dominated the indexes with a gigantic 79 appearances! I was also startled by the absence of the big name player Rio Tinto (RIO) to make the cut in any of the components of the unseen world. I don't follow what I can't see, so these parts are dead meat for me. You can't hit what you can't see and these indexes trade in the shadow world of the OTC.

In the visible world of ETFs, Kinross Gold (KGC) was the dog pound Pit Bull. But the watch dog German Shepherds of the invisible world were the big three of the listed world: Newmont Mining (NEM), Freeport McMoran (FCX) and Barrick Gold Mines (ABX). These are gold mining companies with a rich pedigree.

I don't follow mutual funds, so I have very little to say about them. They are, in fact, the largest components in any computer trading system. They are also the least important. My mom used to say, "if you don't have anything nice to say, shut your trap." So I'll keep my big fat trap shut!

There were some serious short comings with the components line of inquiry. First, and most important, was the absence of Exchange Traded Notes (ETNs) from the components section on Yahoo! Finance ETNs which are debt and not equity, provide all systems with mega leverage plus the rewards of trading to the short side. Second, the Yahoo! Finance components only include those parts who appear in the top ten in terms of ownership. So, if your investment racing Greyhound came in 11th they didn't win, place or show. It also means the visible and invisible electronic worlds may be only the tip of the iceberg of a much larger submerged world.

Before you get your undies in an uproar, there are a number of things to ponder. First, I don't think the invisible world is a part of a grand conspiracy by institutions to cheat the small investor. There are just too many components for any newspaper to publish. The gold system, which is relatively small, has thousands of components.

Next, and most importantly, the two electronics worlds, the visible and invisible, are in fact, the same. They work in concert with each other. When one goes up the other goes up. When one goes down, ditto. They are not mutually exclusive entities who perform behaviorally opposite from one another.

Finally, which gold mining stocks should you follow to monitor both worlds. In the visible world, Kinross Gold (KGC) is still the lead dog. In the invisible cosmos, you have the pick of the litter. Any one of the following: Newmont Mining (NEM), Freeport McMoran (FCX) or Barrick Gold (ABX) would win Best in Show for the invisible world. By following any of these, you can predict the future behavior of the modern gold trading system for the gold mining sector: indexes, ETFs, and mutual funds.

When it comes to trading the bullion sector of the modern gold trading system there isn't any invisible world. What you see if what you get.

The Modern Gold Trading System: The Gold Bullion Sector

The Ignition Points: (1) gold futures prices (CMX) 100 troy ounce contract and (2) algorithmic trading. **NYSE ARCA:** Physical Asian Gold Shares (AGOL), Power Shares DB Gold Fund (DGL), 2X Gold Bull/S&P500 Bear (FSG), SPDR Gold Trust (GLD), iShares Comex Gold Trust (IAU), Physical Swiss Gold Shares (SGOL), Gold Trendpilot ETN(TBAR), UBS E TRACS CMCI Gold

(UBG) and Velocity Shares 3X Gold ETN (UGLD). **Inverse Gold Bullion ETFs:** Velocity Shares Inverse 3X Inverse ETN (300%) DGLD, Pro Shares Ultra Short Gold (200%) GLL, Power Shares DB Gold Double Short ETN (200%) DZZ and Power Shares DB Gold Short ETN (100%) DGZ.

As you can see, the gold mining sector is more complex than the gold bullion system. I prefer the bullion sector over the gold mining sector because it is much easier to read. If gold were to sky rocket, the very first place it will show up is UGLD. To read the system, you have three choices.   One, follow the gold futures. Next, follow GLD bracketed by UGLD and DGLD. Finally, keep an eye on IAU bracketed by UGLD and DGLD. While I am not cheap, I believe in getting value for my money (just one the important lessons I learned from Tom). When you look at apples to apples comparisons of the expense ratios of bullion ETFs, I prefer IAU (expense ration of .25%) to outrageous expense ratios of Mickey Mouse ETFs like TBAR (1.00%) or FSG (.75%).

$10,000 AN OUNCE GOLD: HYPE OR REAL?

In a full page ad, a gold coin seller is urging investors to pay a lot of money ($142.90) for a tiny amount of gold ($5). The central thesis of the ad was the lure of the price of gold sky rocketing to a future price of $10,000 an ounce. Here are the ads main points on the subject of $10,000 an ounce gold: "Gold Around $1,600 PER OZ. EXPERTS PREDICT $10,000 PER OZ." " Gold, which recently skyrocketed past $1,600 per ounce, is predicted by experts to have the explosive upside potential of reaching up to $10,000 per ounce." " With prices currently around $1,600 per ounce, it is critical that individuals move now because as soon as tomorrow, Gold could start its predicted steep rise to $10,000 per ounce."

Who are the "experts" and what do they have to say? To be honest, the names mean absolutely nothing to me. I don't follow them or care what they have to say. When it comes to gold, just like everything else, I think all by my lonesome. Here's the line up and their predictions: John Paulson $ 4,000 an ounce (2013) Peter Cooper ("very conservative forecast") $5,000 an oz., Peter Krauth $5,000 an oz., Rob McEwen $5,000 an oz., Harry Schultz $6,000 per ounce, Alf Field $6,221 per oz., Egon von Greyerz $7,200 per ounce, Arnold Beck " parabolic top of $10,000 oz. by 2012," Larry Edelson $10,000 per oz.(2012-2020), Peter Schiff $10,000 oz., and Shayne McGuire $10,000 per ounce. It is interesting there isn't a woman in the whole cast of $10,000 an ounce prognosticators. I wonder why?

The head cheer leader of the group is Shayne McGuire Of course, McGuire is using the press to pimp his book about $10,000 an ounce gold called "Hard Money." McGuire beats the same drum as all the other "gold bugs" bitten with the $10,000 an ounce disease. The key element that binds these bugs is the specter of supersonic, hyper, parabolic and hyperbolic inflation. It is the "end of the world" scenario, the "Armageddon" scenario, and the "great crash" scenario. The goal is to evoke visions of post WW1 Germany when a loaf of bread cost a wheel barrow of money. It is aimed at elderly well heeled investors. It is a fear appeal message on steroids.

Doctor Doom and the Perfect Storm: 2013

There is another new popular prognosticator of profits and his name is Nouriel Roubini AKA Dr. Doom. He is a NYU professor who successfully predicted the financial crisis in 2008 and he is stepping into the batters box again. Dr. Doom is predicting a perfect storm of bad economic news that will send the global economies into a world wide recession. All of his reasons for the perfect storm will have a direct impact on gold bullion prices.

Dr. Doom gives us fives reasons to buy his premise of a world wide recession. In a report to Reuters, his first reason is the worsening debt crisis in Europe. It isn't just Europe. The entire planet is awash and drowning in debt. It's the California cities of Stockton and San Bernadino (both bankrupt), the US Post Office default on $5.5 billion in debt, and then there are the PIGS (Portugal, Italy, Ireland, Greece and Spain). Quite frankly, I don't think the world can guilt trip (emotionally blackmail) Germany into assuming the responsibility for trillions of dollars of Euro debt. Default in Europe is highly likely in 2013. Score a point for Dr. Doom.

This is a special note of warning about the upcoming debt (bond) crisis. It will be like no other debt crisis in history. The last bear market in bonds happened between 1975-1982. It was a human event. There were no synthetic portfolios, derivatives, or ETFs back then. A bond system collapse will be controlled by the computers and not humans. It will be swift and merciless.

Your biggest problem will be the behavior of your financial adviser. There has been a thirty year secular bull market in bonds. The person who is responsible for your money has zero experience in dealing with a bear market in bonds. Hell, most of them weren't even born in 1975. They will be like deer caught in the headlights of a speeding Porsche. They don't have the emotional make up or the training to handle plunging bond prices. There are two bits of help. First, watch your monthly statements like an eagle. At the first sign of falling bond prices sell and switch to cash. Second, unlike the last bond bear market, in this one, there is a chance to make obscene profits. It can be found in the world of INVERSE bond ETFs like TBT.

Back to Dr, Doom. His next reason for world wide recession are the tax increases and spending cuts in the US. Those gutless creeps in DC have put us all behind the eight ball. These mandatory cuts may cost the US some 700,000 jobs. A lot of those lost jobs will be high paying defense jobs. A big job loss will push US unemployment back up over double digits. Score another point for Dr. Doom. Dr. Doom is predicting a hard landing in China. This one fascinates me. A hard down turn in China will ripple through out the entire planet. A cold in China means the Asian flu for everyone else. I am very curious how the Red Communist Party will deal with an unhappy Chinese middle class? Mao forced them into the rice paddies where they died by the millions in the last Red Revolution. How will Beijing react? Score a half point for Dr. Doom.

Dr. Doom is predicting a further slowing in the emerging markets. For gold bullion, an decline in the booming market in India will spell big problems for the yellow metal. There is a contagion effect and Dr. Doom gets another point.

The first four reasons presented by Dr. Doom, all point to lower gold bullion prices world wide. The biggest single enemy of gold bullion prices is deflation. The engine for gold bullion growth has been the wild spending sprees by both China and India. When consumers become paranoid, the first thing to go are the luxury items. Things like gold jewelery.

There is a fifth reason for Dr. Doom's perfect storm and it is the joker the in the deck. The wild card. He is predicting a military confrontation with Iran. I don't know why he doesn't call a spade a spade. The central question is, will Israel attack Iran to prevent them from going nuclear? Based on history, the answer is undeniably, YES. Israel attacked Iraq and Syria to crush their nuclear program ambitions and she will do the same against Iran. The question isn't "if" but "when"? An attack could send oil and gold prices into the stratosphere. For me, the question becomes, what will Pakistan do?

The Rear View Mirror:2012

In 2012, the performance of the modern gold trading system was the tale of two investment cities. It was the worst of times and the most mediocre of times. For one, it was a story of agonizing financial pain. For the other, it was a time of middle of the road gains.

For the investor who owned gold mining stocks, 2012 was a brutal year. As part of the S&P Dow Jones Industry Groups, the gold mining sector dropped by -14.93% in 2012. Only three sectors (alternative fuels, renewable energy equipment, and electronic equipment) did worse.

The PHLX Gold/Silver Index lost -8.3% for the year. An eagle eyed investor might ask why the difference between the Philly Index and the gold mining sector? The PHLX Gold/ Silver Index was enhanced by the sterling performance of silver mining stocks, who were up double digits for the year.

There were gargantuan losses by the big names in the gold mining sector of the larger system. They were: Anglo Gold Ashanti (AU) -26.1%, Barrick Gold (ABX) -22.6%, El Dorado Gold (EGO) -17.1%, Freeport McMoran (FCX) -6.1%, Gold Fields ADS (GFI) -18.1%, Gold Corp (GG) -17.1%, Iam Gold (IAG) -27.1%, Kinross Gold (KGC) -14.7% and Newmont Mines (NEM) -22.6%. Ugly,ugly and more ugly! These results could have been much worse. These year ending figures were aided by the nearly 30% bounce off the bottom new 52 week lows that lasted for five months, January to May 2012.

The second tier gold mining stocks were unmercifully hammered in 2012. The junior varsity gold mining stocks were slammed very hard. Those stocks who got crucified by the market were: Entree Gold (EGI) -61.7%, Lakeshore Gold (LSG) -40.1%, Minoco Gold (MGH) –40.6%, and Nova Gold Resources (NVG)-41.1%. I believe this damage was caused more by the lack of liquidity than poor management. These stocks always rise higher and more dramatically than their bigger counterparts. They also crash faster than the varsity gold mining stocks. This is truly a case of buyer beware. For these babies, it's early in and early out!

Believe it or not, there were some pretty sizable winners in the gold mining sector. There is a silver lining in every disaster. The big winners were: Aurico Gold (AUQ) +2.1%, Rio Tinto ADS (RIO) +18.7%, Seabridge Gold (SA) +11.5%, Yamana Gold (AUY) +17.2%, Royal Gold (RGLD) +20.7%, Central Gold Trust (GTU) +9.4%, and New Gold (NGD) +9.4%. Overall, the losers swamped the winners. Quite frankly, I don't have the skill set to pick a small stream of winners in an Amazon river of losers. The winners may have been diversified into silver and copper. Other winners may have increased their gold reserves either by discovery or merger?

The gold mining sector ETF components was an absolute disaster in 2012. There were massive losses which are in concert with the gigantic losses in the indexes and stocks It was a symphony of negative congruence. The big losers were: Global Gold Explorers (GLDX) -31.9%, iShs MSCI Global Gold Miners (RING) -24.3%, Global X Pure Gold Miners (GGGG) -14.5%, Market Vector Gold Miners (GDX) -9.8%, and DXDNDLYGLDMNR3XBULL (NUGT) -26%.

There were ZERO winners in the gold mining ETF sector. The most puzzling of the lot was the inverse twin to NUGT, DXNDLYGLDMNR3XBEAR (DUST) with a mirror loss of -26%. For five months, DUST was the stock cock of the walk. The big rooster in the hen house with a string of new impressive 52 week highs. Once the five month bear raid was over, DUST plummeted. Both DUST and NUGT ended the year with identical -26% losses. They should have been more balanced with one winning 26% and the other losing 26%. I stay awake at nights trying to untangle the reasons why.

Now, let's turn to the gold bullion component of the system. The trading range for yellow metal was a low of $1536.20 an ounce and a high of $1794.10 an ounce. For the year, gold was up a wimp meter of just 6.96%. This is the smallest amount of price appreciation since the market disaster of 2008. Gold bullion got beat by just about all the major stock indexes. The DJIA was up +7.3%, the Nasdaq 100 up +16.8%, the S&P 500 up +13.4%, and the Russell 2000 up +14.6%. Clearly, there were more reward than risk for stocks than for commodities. IF you owned stock indexes, you would have avoided the agony of gold ownership. Would have, could have, should have. Ah, the genius of 20/20 hindsight!

Since the news for gold bullion was positive, there were 100% winners in the long position gold bullion ETFs. It was a concerto of positive harmony. The winners were: ETFS Asian Gold (AGOL) + 6.6%, ETRACS Gold (UBG) +6.1%, ETFS Gold Trust (SGOL) + 6.6%, iShs Gold (IAU) + 6.9%, SPDR Gold Trust (GLD) +6.6%, Pro Shares Ult Gold (UGL) +8%, Power Shares DB Dbl Long (DGP) +9.3%, Power Shares DB Gold (DGL) +5.3%, and VS3XGold (UGLD) +8.3%.

The losers were 100% of the universe of inverse gold bullion ETFs. Due to leverage, some losses were significantly larger than others. Let this be a learning moment for you. What ever the rewards of the leverage, the penalties for being wrong are much harsher. The losers were: Power Shares DB Dbl Short (DZZ) -17.9%, Power Shares DB Gold Short ETN (DGZ) -8.4%, Pro Shares Ult Short Gold (GLL) – 21.1%, and VS3X INVERSE GOLD (DGLD) -26.5%. Good, this is a system in perfect negative agreement.

As we began to transition from 2012 to 2013, there were some aspects of the modern gold trading system that bothered me to no end. First, given the punch of Qualitative Easing Three (QE3), gold bullion should have traded higher. Second, given the absolutely putrid performance of the US dollar, gold bullion should have traded higher. Third, given the stubborn high price of oil, particularly in a world wide soft economy, gold bullion should have traded higher. Finally, gold mining stocks are closer to their 52 week lows than their old 52 week highs, giving me a case of the chilly willys. I don't like the feeling I have about the system and its future performance.

What's an investor to do when the entire system is a boiling cauldron of neutrality? There are NO buy signals and NO sell signals. He prudent investor who is willing to underwrite risk in an uncertain market should fall back to the conservative stance of selling covered calls for protection. The lessons to be learned from the performance of the modern gold trading system in 2012 are manifold. First, and most importantly, the system went down right on cue when it was supposed to. Conversely, the bullion section of the system, went up just like it was ordained. This should be a confidence builder to the novice systems reader.

Second, we just have to deal with the sales myth that gold mining stocks are the "safe and conservative " alternative to the risks of gold bullion ownership. For decades, gullible elderly investors have been badly burned by this sales baloney. The data from 2012 tells a completely different story as gold mining stocks lost -15% while gold bullion was up +7%! According to one "expert", the long term trend holds true to the 2012 model of behavior. During the years between 2002 and 2012, gold bullion appreciated by a mind blowing +425% while gold mining rose by +125%. Incredibly, the "expert" recommended buying gold mining stocks on the theory they were poised to play catch up. According to the great American philosopher, Forrest Gump, "stupid is as stupid does." Sometimes. I don't know whether to laugh or cry at the recommendations of the so called "experts"? Maybe, the smart thing to do is own $2 in gold bullion ETFs for every 50 cents of gold mining stocks?

Just for kicks, the performance of oil during 2012 was the exact opposite the gold mining system. The commodity of crude oil went down-7.1% while the oil companies were up marginally by an average of +2%. After all, gas stations are really 7-11's in disguise. I am so old, I remember when you could actually buy tires, get an oil change, have your brakes fixed and get an engine over haul at your local gas station. Now it's all beer, potato chips and hot dogs. A slice of Americana lost forever.

Case History #12:
The Eve of Destruction: February 2013

For gold owners, both holding long positions in gold mining stocks and bullion, February 20th and 21st were two days of pure hell on earth. It is almost unbelievable that after a mere ten months that the longs are being molested by the shorts again. This assault is different from the previous one that lasted from January 2012 thru May. That abuse, in my opinion, was the result of market manipulation. A great bear raid like from the 1920's. The new attack is from purely market forces, the plummeting value of gold bullion. The appetite for all things gold is wane and weak.

On February 20th, thirteen components of the gold mining sector of the modern gold trading system violated new 52 low week territory. It is fascinating that unless you are a big name like Apple (AAPL) no body seems interested in reporting on new 52 week lows. Those parts were: the PHLX Gold/Silver Index hits a new 52 week low of 134.57 D. For the year,so far, the index is down -18.7%. A 20% decline is the classic signal for a bear market. Will anyone notice? Other components who were compromised were: Anglo Ashanti (AU) 24.70 D, Barrick Gold (ABX) 24.70D, El Dorado Gold (EGO) 9.40D, Gold Fields ADS (GFI) 10.31 D, Newmont Mines (NEM) 40.56D, Harmony Gold (HMY) 6.23D, and I am Gold (IAG) 7.40 D.

Of course, there was a ripple effect from the indexes and stocks directly to the ETFs. Gold mining ETFs were soundly ravished by the sellers. The new 52 week lows were: DXN DLY 3X BULL (NUGT) 5.55D, iShsMSCI Global Gold Miners (RING) 16.00D, Market Vectors Gold (GDX) 37.39D, and Market Vector Junior Gold (GDXJ) 15.74D. The fact that the PHLX Gold/Silver Index and

Market Vector Gold (GDX) are crashing to new 52 week lows spells BIG trouble for this part of the system. This is a replay of last year.

Gold futures for bullion were compromised by sellers and lost $26 a contract to close at 1,577.60 a new six month low. Gangs of sellers pushed gold bullion to an inter day low of 1,561.80 just a mere away 25.60 from a new 52 week low. Accordingly, the extremely leveraged VS 3X Gold (UGLD) hit an initial new 52 week low at 33.35 D. This is an important development. The chances that UGLD will hit another new 52 week low are exceptionally high. These things seem to assume a life of their own. With the odds saying UGLD will achieve another new 52 week low being 99 out of 100, UGLD is showing signs of morphing into a SELL signal. The next day, February 21st, ten components of the system penetrated the new 52 week low mark. The losers were: ASA 19.00D, Anglo Ashanti Pfd A (AU PrA) 30.34D, Barrick Gold (ABX) 30.20D, Gold Fields ADS (GFI) 8.56D and I am Gold (IAG) 7.27D.

The ETF's who broached new 52 week low territory were: Glb X Gold Miners (GLDX) 5.30D, Global X Jr Gold Miners (JUNR) 7.92D, Global X Pure Gold Miners (GGGG) 8.39D, iShsMSCI Global Gold Miners (RING) and Market Vector Jr Gold Miners (GDXJ) 15.68D. All in all, the gold mining sector of the modern gold trading system, is showing signs of extreme stress.

Case History# 13
February 28th,2013: The System is Burnt Toast

The numbers always tell the truth. In this case, they are predicting bad vibes for the long positions in the gold mining sector of the modern gold trading system. The PHLX Gold/Silver Index continues its slide. It closed at 134.40D, another new 52 week low. For the year, the index has fallen by 18.9%. Gold futures (CMX)100 oz contract shed -17.50 to close at 1,557.70.

The system yielded 12 new 52 week lows. They were: ASA 18.84D, Anglo Gold Ashanti ADS (AU) 24.17D,Anglo Gold Ashanti ADS Pfd A (AuPrA) 29.06D, Gold Fields (GFI) 8.27D, Harmony Gold (HMY) 6.13D, I am Gold (IAG) 6.68D, Newmont Mine (NEM) 40.13D, Sibanye Gold (SBGL) 5.64D, DXN DLY 3X Miner BULL (NUGT) 5.64D, Glb X Gold Exp (GLDX) 5.21D, Glb X Jr Miners (JUNR) 7.91D, and Market Vector Gold (GDX) 37.72D.

The most interesting aspect of this day is the performance of Factor Gold Bull/S&P 500 Bear (FSG). FSG is a bullion based ETF and its poor performance should be a lesson for everyone. In this case, bullion went down and the S&P 500 went up, totally destroying the whole idea behind this investment. When it comes to investing, whatever you think is impossible is in reality, highly probable.

The Last Picture Show: No Mas

Every project has a position where you reach the point of diminishing returns. We are at that very point right now. This is the last picture show. By now, you should be able to close your eyes, concentrate, and see what is happening in your minds eye. There is a deluge of new 52 week lows in the gold mining sector. It's a flood of bad news for the long positions. It starts with the PHLX Gold/ Silver Index reaching yet another new 52 week low closing at 134.4D. For the year, the index is down 18.9%. This is,by far, the worse performing index in the WSJ. Gold bullion fares little better. The Gold futures contract (CMX) 100 oz dumps -17.50 a contract closing at 1577.70. Gold's failure to hold 1,600 an ounce spells T-R-O-U-B-L-E!

The system is submerged under an ocean of new 52 week lows. The losers are: ASA 18.71D, Anglo Gold Ashanti (AU) 23.88D, Anglo Gold Ashanti Pfd A (AUPrA) 28.49D, Barrick Gold (ABX) 29.33D, Gold Fields (GFI) 8.12D, I am Gold (IAG) 6.51D, Newmont Mining (NEM) 39.56D, Seabridge Gold (SA) 12,01D, Entree Gold (EGI) .39 and Lakeshore Gold (LSG) .54.

The NYSE Arca sends us: DXNDLYGLDMNR3XBULL (NUGT) 5.35D, Glb X Gold Explorers (GLDX) 5.12D, Glb Gold Jr Miners (JUNR) 7.64D, Glb X Pure Gold Mns (GGGG) 8.30D, iShs MSCI Glb Gold Miners (RING) 15.80D, Market Vector Gold (GDX) 37.02D, and Market Vector Jr Gold (GDXJ) 15.55D. I think if I was the busiest person in the world and wanted to keep my finger on the pulse of the gold mining sector of the modern gold trading system, I'd place my thumb on Market Vector Gold (GDX). It's simply a gold mine of information, the mother lode of all the data. For the true gold bug, when it comes to bullion, the center of that universe is the Gold futures (CMX) 100 oz contract. In the bullion portion of the system, I like iShs Gold (IAU) as a barometer of price/market change.

Your Final Examination:The Modern Gold Trading System

This near the end of the line. There are no more case histories or picture shows. By now, you have seen a nearly balanced number of the systems performance in a raging bull and two very nasty bear markets. The only way to gauge whether you have absorbed the mechanics of how the system works is by a final examination. I am an educator, so what else would you expect?

All of the data for the final come from a real life source, The Wall Street Journal. There are no hypothetical XYZ corporations in this test. Good luck and be careful!

1. In a bull market cycle, the long positions increase in value and the short positions decrease?

          T   F

2. In a bull market cycle, the long positions decrease and the short positions increase?

          T   F

3. In a bull market cycle, the aggressive investor, will be long which of the following?

          a. puts

          b. calls

4. On Monday. April 15, 2013, the PHLX Gold/Silver index fell to a new 52 week low (D). This means all of the gold mining ETFs traded lower?

          T   F

5. In a bear market cycle, the long positions increase and the shorts decrease?

          T   F

6. In a bear market cycle, the long positions decrease and the shorts increase?

          T   F

7. In a bear market cycle, the aggressive investor will be long which of the following?

          a. calls

          b. puts

8. Market Vector Gold (GDX) traded to a new 52 week low @ $28.99(D) a share on April 15, 2013. The means it's leveraged derivatives, DXNDLYGLDMNR3XBEAR (DUST) traded to a new 52 week low (D) and DXNDLYGLDMNR3XBULL (NUGT) traded to a new 52 week high?

        T   F

9. For the year, the PHLX Gold/Silver index is down -36.3%, this means the index is in a **bull market?**

        T   F

10. For the year, the PHLX Gold/Silver index is down -36.3%, this means the index is in a **bear market?**

        T   F

11. In a bull market for gold mining, you want to be long DXNDLYGLD-MNR3XBULL (NUGT) ?

        T   F

12. In a bull market for gold mining, you want to be short DXNDLYGLD-MNR3XBULL (NUGT) ?

        T   F

13. In a bear market for gold mining, you want to be long DXNDLYGLD-MNR3XBEAR (DUST) ?

        T   F

14. In a bear market for gold mining, you want to be short DXNDLY-GLDMNR3XBEAR (DUST) ?

        T   F

15. Which of the following gives you the most information about the gold mining sector of the modern gold trading system?

        a. iSHS Gold (IAU)

        b. Market Vector Jr. Gold (GDXJ)

        c. SPDR Gold Tr (GLD)

        d. Market Vector Gold (GDX)

On Monday, April 15, 2013, the PHLX Gold/Silver index fell to a new 52 week low @ 105.23D. Which of the following statements are true?

16. DXNDLYGLDMNR3XBEAR (DUST) gained +$22.66 a share for a one day gain of 29.03%. For the year, DUST is up +107.3%.

        T   F

17. VS 3X Inverse Gold (DGLD) gained $14.59 a share for a one day gain of +25.09%. For the year DGLD is up +52.3%.

        T   F

18. Pro Shs DB Double Short Gold (DZZ) lost -$6.36 a share for a one day loss of -14.91%. For the year, DZZ is down -34.7%.

        T   F

19. Pro Shs DB Gold Dbl Long (DGP) gained +$ 7.65 a share for a one day gain of +18.9%. For the year, DGP is up +36.4%.

        T   F

20. DXNDLYGLDMNR3XBULL (NUGT) lost -$4.94 a share for a one day loss of -29.6%. For the year, NUGT is down -82.5%.

        T   F

21. On April 19,2013, Goldman Sachs (GS) advised their clients to short iShs Gold (IAU) predicting lower gold bullion prices. GS expects IAU to increase in value?

        T   F

22. GS is predicting which type of market cycle for gold bullion?

        a. bull   b. bear

23. GS could have advised their clients to short which of the following groups?

    a. Apple (AAPL),Bank of America (BAC), Coca Cola (KO) and Microsoft (MSFT).

    b. Glb X Gold Exp (GLDX), Glb X Jr. Gold Exp (JUNR), Market Vector Gold (GDX), and DXNDLYGLDMNR3XBULL (NUGT).

    c. ETFS Gold Tr (SGOL), Pwr Shs DB 2X Long ETN (DGP), SPDR Gold Tr (GLD) and VS 3X Gold (UGLD).

24. GS could have advised their clients to take a long position in which of the following?

    a. Pwr Shs DB Dbl Short Gold ETN (DZZ), PwrShsDBShort ETN (DGZ), Pro Shs Ult Short Gold (GLL) and VS 3X Inverse Gold (DGLD).

    b. Apple (AAPL), Bank of America (BAC), Coca Cola (KO), and Microsoft (MSFT).

    c. Glb X Gold Exp (GLDX), Glb X Jr. Gold Exp (JUNR), Market Vector Gold (GDX), DXNDLYGLDMNR3XBULL (NUGT).

25. When gold bullion prices increase, you want to be long which of the following?
    a. DXNDLYGLDMNR3XBEAR (DUST)
    b. DXNDLYGLDMNR3XBULL (NUGT)
    c. VS 3X Gold (UGLD).
26. When gold bullion prices decrease, you want to be long which of the following?
    a. VS 3X Inverse Gold (DGLD)
    b. VS 3X Gold (UGLD)
    c. Market Vector Gold (GDX)
    d. all of the above

27 Which of the following is the best source about gold bullion market cycles?
    a. Kinross Gold (KGC)
    b. Barrick Gold (ABX)
    c. Gold futures (CMX) 100 oz contract
    d. Market Vector Gold (GDX)
28. In the gold mining sector, during a bull market, there is a concert of new 52 week highs in the long positions of the indexes, gold mining ETFs and gold mining stocks?

    T   F

29. In the gold mining sector, during a bull market, there is a concert of new 52 week lows in the long positions of the indexes, gold mining ETFs, and gold mining stocks?

    T   F

30. In the gold mining sector, during a bear market, there is a concert of new 52 week highs in the short positions of the indexes and gold mining ETFs?

    T   F

31. In the gold mining sector, during a bear market, there is a concert of new 52 week lows in the short positions of the indexes and gold mining ETFs?

    T   F

On Monday, April 15,2013, gold bullion was battered by a perfect storm of bad news. A terrorist attack in Boston, lower growth reports from China, increased gold import taxes in India, banking woes in Cyprus, poor recent demand for bullion all conspired to send gold bullion down to a new two year low. The gold futures contract (CMX) 100 oz settled @ $1,360.60D, down a massive- $140.40. This is the worst drubbing for gold since the bad old days of 1983. This was a day for the history books..

Mark each of the following components either a new 52 week high (U) or new 52 week low (D).

32. ETFS Asian Gold	AGOL	_____
33. ETRACS Gold	UBG	_____
34. ETFS Gold Tr	SGOL	_____
35 Factor 2X Gold/S&P	FS.G	_____
36. iShs Gold	IAU	_____
37. Pwr Shs DB Dbl Long Gold	DGP	_____
38. Pwr Shs DB Gold	DGL	_____
39. Pwr Shs DB Dbl Short	DZZ	_____
40. Pwr Shs DB Gold Short	DGZ	_____
41. Pro Shs Ult Gold	UGZ	_____
42. Pro Shs Ult Short Gold	GLL	_____
43. SPDR Gold Tr	GLD	_____
44. Sprott Physical Gold	PHYS	_____
45. VS 3X Gold	UGLD	_____
46. VS 3X Inverse Gold	DGLD	_____

47. In the gold bullion sector, during a bull market, there is a concert of new 52 week highs in the long positions of the gold futures and gold bullion ETFs?

        T   F

48. In the gold bullion sector, during a bull market, there is a concert of new 52 week lows in the short positions of the gold futures and gold bullion ETFs?

        T   F

49. In the gold bullion sector, during a bear market, there is a concert of new 52 week highs in the short positions of the gold futures and gold bullion ETFs?

    T   F

50. In the gold bullion sector, during a bear market, there is a concert of new 52 week lows in the short positions of the gold futures and gold bullion ETFs?

    T   F

As gold bullion prices crashed, gold miners around the world were devastated. The PHLX Gold/Silver index closed @ 105.23D, a new 52 week low. The index lost $11.34 for a one day loss of -9.59%. For the year, the index is down -36.3%. Of all the indexes in the <u>WSJ</u>, this is the worst performer of all.

Mark each of the following components either a new 52 week high (U) or new 52 week low (D). Let's start with the NYSE.

51. ASA Prec Mtls   ASA   _____
52. Alamos Gold   AGI   _____
53. Anglo Ashanti Gold ADS   AU   _____
54. Anglo Ashanti Gold PrA ADS   AUPrA   _____
55. Aurico Gold   AUQ   _____
56. Barrick Gold   ABX   _____
57. El Dorado Gold   EGO   _____
58. Frpt McCG   FCX   _____
59. Gold Fields   GFI   _____
60. Gold Corp   GG   _____
61. Harmony Gold   HMY   _____
62. I am Gold   IAG   _____
63. Kinross Gold   KGC   _____
64. Newmont Mng   NEM   _____
65. Seabridge Gold   SA   _____
66. Sibayne Gold   SBGL   _____
67. Yamana Gold   AUY   _____

The NYSE Arca

68. Glb X Gold Exp   GLDX   _____
69. Glb X Jr Gold Exp   JUNR   _____

70. iShs MSCI Glb Gld Mnrs	RING	_____
71. Market Vector Gold	GDX	_____
72. Market Vector Jr Gold	GDXJ	_____
73. DXNDLYGLDMNR3XBULL	NUGT	_____
74. DXNDLYGLDMNR3XBEAR	DUST	_____

The NYSE MARKET

75. Allied NV Gold	ANV	_____
76. Asanko Gold	AKG	_____
77. Brigus Gold	BRD	_____
78. Central Gold Tr	GTU	_____
79. Gold Res	GORO	_____
80. Gld Std Vrt	GSY	_____
81. Golden Minerals	AUMN	_____
82. Lake Shore Gold	LSG	_____
83. Midway Gold	MDW	_____
84. Minoco Gold	MGH	_____
85. New Gold	NGD	_____
86. Nova Gold	NG	_____
87. Sand Storm Gold	SAND	_____
88. Vista Gold	VGI	_____

The NASDAQ

89. Credit Suisse Gold	GLDI	_____
90. Rangold Res ADS	GOLD	_____
91. Royal Gold	RGLD	_____

This is the end of part one of your final examination. Part two will be found at the end of the next chapter. The key will be found after the next chapter.

The Modern Silver Trading System

From antiquity to the present hour, there has always been a close and cozy relationship between gold and silver. In nature, where you find one, the other is close by. They are compadres on the Table of Periodic Elements. Silver lives due north of gold. In the investment universe, gold and silver tend to trend in the same price direction. Usually gold is the head and silver is the tail. In 2012, their roles were reversed. Silver bullion performed slightly better than gold. The silver miners clobbered gold bullion by a country mile.

In the cosmos of computers, gold and silver are separate but not completely mutually exclusive systems. They are structured exactly the same. Each system has a mining and bullion sector. They always behave exactly the same. In a bull market, the long positions go up and the short positions go down. It's the law. In a bull market, there is a consensus of new 52 week highs in all the long position components. It's the law.

In a bear market, there is a consonance of new 52 week lows in all the long positions, and all the inverse short positions climb to new 52 week highs. It's the law. This is true for everything that involves computers and investments. It's the law for everything in computer land and there are no exceptions. None.

It's Time for a Pop Quiz

Let's make a point, create a learning moment, and test your skills with a pop quiz. The following data comes from my universe for equities and ETFs for 2013. All the numbers come from Yahoo! Anyone can go online and replicate my world. The quiz covers equities in the current bull market and different classes of investments, mining, bullion, and currencies, in a bear market. Please mark each of the following system components either a new 52 week high (U) or a new 52 week low (D). The numbers in ( ) is the total number of new weekly highs or new weekly lows. At the time of the quiz, there had been a total of 16 weeks.

The Bull Market of 2013

1. Pro Shs Ult Dow 30 (13)   DDM   _____
2. Pro Shs Ult Short Dow 30 (14)   DXD   _____
3. Pro Shs Ult Russell 2000 (9)   UWM   _____
4. Pro Shs Ult Short Russell 2000 (10) RWM   _____
5. ProShs Ult Pro S&P 500 (11)   UPRO   _____
6. Pro Shs Ult Short Pro S&P 500 (13) SPXU   _____

The Bear Market of 2013

7. DXNDLYGLDMNR3XBULL (6)   NUGT   _____
8. DXNDLYGLDMNR3XBEAR (1)   DUST   _____
9. VS 3X Inverse Gold (3)   UGLD   _____

10. VS 3X Gold (1)	DGLD	_____
11. Pro Shs Ult Short Yen (11)	YCS	_____
12. Pro Shs Ult Yen (13)	YCL	_____
13. VS 3X Silver (3)	USLV	_____
14. VS 3X Inverse Silver	DSLV	_____

How sweet of a world is this? Can it get any better? I hope even the most jaded cynic on the planet appreciates the symmetry of the different systems.

Of course, if the index futures, indexes and ETFs (long) are making new 52 week highs so must by law, should a group of individual stocks trading in the stratosphere of new 52 week highs. In my world, new 52 week highs out weigh new 52 week lows by ten tons. Those long stocks who populate my world making new 52 week highs in 2013 are: T (2), AMZN (3), AXP (9), BAC (6), BA (4), CVX (4), KO (5), DIS (9), GE (3), GOOG (5), HD (7), IBM (1), JNJ (14). MSFT (2), PFE (10), PG (10), WMT (3), and YHOO (13). My favorite is YHOO who started its run in late 2012 at near $17 a share and is pushing the $25 a share level. I can't find a single expert who has any good to say about YHOO!

There were only two resident's of the Heart Break Hotel of new 52 week lows: AAPL (3) and SLW (1). Sadness for the longs, elation for the shorts. This is the reality of the world in which we live.

Hi-Ho-Silver

I have never been all that gung ho about silver as an investment. For me, its always been a matter of marketing hype versus substance. The mantra has always been that silver is a cheap substitute for gold. A sales campaign for investors with champagne tastes on a beer budget. Well, just because some thing appears to be cheap, it docsn't mean that it is valuable. Just ask the Hunt brothers of Dallas, Texas about "cheap" silver. Investors tend to over bet on cheap silver! It's a sales trap with a lot of sex appeal.

While gold and silver trading systems behave exactly the same. There are some sharp and importance differences between them. These differences may be critical to your future net worth. The first difference is size. Gold is a monster compared to silver. Take a look at the size comparisons between gold, silver and just one component of the Dow 30, IBM. Please remember, only the mining sectors lend themselves to a fair comparison.

Part	Index Futures	Indexes	ETFs	Mutual Funds
Gold	0	165	42	1,113
Silver	0	106	12	56
IBM	4	49	63	1,139

When it comes to size of the components, remember there aren't 106 indexes in the silver mining sector. One hundred and six is the sum total of the ten largest holdings. In reality, the largest number of indexes that any one mining stock belongs to is in the low 40's. The comparison show that just one part of the Dow 30, IBM, is larger than the totality of either gold or silver. Just imagine how massive and complex the Dow 30 is if you connect all of the parts? Just for fun, I hooked up all of the Dow 30 indexes together. The results looked like a Rorschach test on steroids. Think about how massive and complex the S&P 500 or Russell 2000 are?

My beef with the silver mining sector has absolutely nothing to do with its size. There are smaller systems than silver miners that I do like. My concerns about the silver mining sector have everything to do with the composition and quality of its parts. The silver mining sector is as muddy and polluted as one of the world's dirtiest rivers, the Rio Grande. On the other hand, the gold mining sector is as clear and pristine as the 1950's Lake Tahoe. The difference between the two reside in the components of the indexes and ETFs of the silver mining sector. For starters, there isn't any silver mining index. None. In the visible world, all we can see are the PHLX Gold/Silver Index and the Amex BUGS Index. Each index has a tiny portion, three silver miners, in their indexes out of a total of sixteen stocks. The percentage of participation are so small that these pee wee league players are contaminants rather than contributors. Without an index exclusively of big and mid size silver miners, I am simply not interested. I wish the big two indexes, the PHLX Gold/Silver and the Amex BUGS would expel the three pollutants and become pure gold miners. Don't hold your breath. I can't think of any other business that is so wedded to tradition than Wall Street. The current indexes are neither fish nor fowl.

My displeasure with the silver mining sector extends to it's ETFs. There isn't a single short (inverse) player, leveraged or not, in the whole stinking universe. This means that the only way to profit from the fall of silver miners is to actually short the stock. Who is your circle of family and friends know how to do that? Poor old GI Joe is shut out of the game and is restricted to making money only when the miners are on a hot streak in the long position. If there isn't any way to play the short side, I am totally uninterested.

Second, there isn't a silver mining ETF that approaches the elegance or diversity of Market Vectors Gold (GDX). None. Not in the same zip code, the same city, the same county, the same state, the same country, the same planet, or the same universe. None. In my opinion, the three main silver mining ETFs: Silver Miners (SIL), iShs MSCI Global Silver Miners (SLVP), and Pure Funds ISE Jr. Silver Miners (small cap)(SILJ) simply don't make the cut. The problem? SIL is just 12% US silver miners and 88% international silver miners. Both SLVP and SILJ are 100% international silver miners. This means that not only do you have to worry about silver bullion prices but the effects that foreign foreign currency translations will have on the bottom line Given the pathetic performance of the US dollar this might be a positive thing. I like things to be simple and this isn't simple.

The Worst ETF in the World?

There is a subculture of investors who absolutely love small cap stocks. I am not nor have I ever been one. For me, the small caps are so sensitive to market conditions, that I don't like the time it takes to keep on top of them. In my opinion, the risks of owning Pure Funds ISE Jr. Silver Miners (small cap) ETF (SILJ) far outweigh the rewards. I'm beginning to think I don't want to own anything with the word "junior" in it! This includes Market Vector Gold Jr. Gold Miners (GDXJ).

The top ten holdings for SILJ are: Mag Silver Corp (MVG.TO), Fortuna Silver Miner (FSM.TO), Mandalay Resources (MND.TO), Endeavor Silver Corp (EXK.TO), G-Resources Grp (OISI.HK), Silver Corp Metals (SVM.TO), Gabriel Res (GBRF.TO), Orko Silver (OKOFF.TO), Aurcana Corp (AUWFF.TO) and Bear Creek Mining Corp (BCEKF.TO). There isn't a single NYSE, NYSE Market, or NASDAQ listed stock in the whole bunch. Tell me, quick, what do you know about the Toronto or Hong Kong exchanges?

If beauty is truly in the eye of the beholder, then there is someone out there, who sees this as a Picasso. In my mind's eye, it is an ugly, ugly, double ugly mess. This one is a dog. A rabid dog just waiting to turn Ma and Pa into dog food.

The Pygmy World of the Silver Mining Sector

This is the universe we can see everyday in the <u>Wall Street Journal</u> or online at Yahoo! To qualify for this pee wee universe, a silver mining stock, had to belong to at least two indexes or ETFs. Those system components are: the PHLX Gold/Silver Index (XAU), the Amex BUGS Index (HUI), the Silver Miners ETF (SIL) or the iShs MSCI Global Silver Miners ETF (SLVP)

Stock	System Membership
Buenaventura (BVN)	XAU, HUI, SLVP
Cour D'Alene Mine (CDE)	SIL, SLVP
First Majestic Silver (AG)	SIL, SLVP
Fresnillo PLC (FES)	SIL, SLVP
Hecla Mining PLC (HL)	HUI, SIL
Hochchild PLC (HOC)	SIL, SLVP
Industria PenolesSAB (PE)	SIL, SLVP
Pan American Silver (PAAS)	XAU, SIL, SLVP
Silver Wheaton (SLW)	XAU, HUI, SIL, SLVP

Without a doubt, just like Kinross Gold (KG) was the king of the visible gold mining sector, Silver Wheaton (SLW) is the ruling monarch of the silver mining cosmos. SLW was also, by a large margin, the largest percentage portion of all the parts of this sector. If you own SLW, you own the silver mining world.

The only part of the silver mining sector I harvest weekly data on is SLW. I am always looking forward and I am thinking about dumping SLW in favor of Southwest Airlines (LUV) in 2014.

The Invisible Modern Silver Trading System

Exactly like the modern gold trading system, there is an invisible, unseen world of silver mining components found on Yahoo!

Stock	Indexes	ETFs	Mutual Funds
BVN	6	0	28
CDE	41	1	0
AG	1	2	0
FES	3	2	0
HL	35	1	2
HOC	3	2	0
PAAS	13	2	6
SLW	4	2	22
TOTAL	106	12	56

The czars of this kingdom are clearly Hecla Mining (HL) and Cour D'Alene (CDE). There doesn't appear to be much of an appetite for the silver miners in the land of mutual funds.

The Silver Bullion Sector

Just like the gold bullion sector, I love the silver bullion sector with equal passion. The silver bullion sector is pure, transparent and highly predictable. In short, it is an easy system to read. You start with the futures and just follow the electrical path through out the bullion based ETFs. The mother lode for data miners is the NYSE Arca. All the bullion ETFs are there: the long and inverse shorts, and gold and silver players. It is, without a doubt, my absolute favorite part of the WSJ.

While the silver bullion sector is smaller than gold, in this case, smaller is just as good. On a Saturday morning basis, I cull the weekly high, low and close for the following bullion parts. They are: iShs Silver Trust (SLV), VS 3X Silver (USLV) and VS 3X Inverse Silver (DSLV).

Final Examination, Part 2
The Bullion Sector of the Modern Silver Trading System

On Monday, April 15, 2013, there was a massive sell off in both sectors of the modern silver trading system. The PHLX Gold/Silver Index closed @ 105.23 D, a new week 52 week low. Of course, there were numerous new 52 week lows among the silver miners. The long silver futures contracts (CMX) 5,000 troy ounces were crucified by sellers. The contract lost -$2.97 to close @ $23.36D, a new 52 week low. Mark each of the following bullion components either a new 52 week high or new 52 week low (D).

92. Pro Shs Ultra Short Silver (ZSL)   _____
93. VS 3X Inverse Silver (DSLV)   _____
94. ETRACS Silver (USV)   _____
95. ETFS Silver Trust (SIVR)   _____
96. iShs Silver Trust (SLV)   _____
97. Pwr Shs DB Silver (AGQ)   _____
98. Sprott Physical Silver (PSLV)   _____
99. VS 3X Silver (USLV)   _____

100. All bullion ETFs (gold&silver), both long and inverse short positions, can be found on which of the following exchanges?
a. NYSE
b. NYSE Market
c. NYSE Arca
d. NASDAQ

With 1 being lowest and 10 being highest, rate your confidence levels in the following skills.

My confidence level in reading and understanding systems behavior?
1   2   3   4   5   6   7   8   9   10

My confidence level in making investment decisions using systems behavior data?
1   2   3   4   5   6   7   8   9   10

At first, I was extremely angry with myself for including silver data in the first case studies. It was so easy collecting data for both gold and silver at the same time. They always appeared in my sources in exactly the same places. I knew they were different systems and figured that I would untangle them somewhere down the road. In retrospect, I should have ignored the silver data. After all, this was a book about gold.

I very briefly thought about going back and deleting everything silver. I was raised better than that. My science mentors, Dr. Dick Hill, Dr. Brad Lashbrook, and Dr. Jim McCroskey, instilled in me a passion to always do the right thing when it came to data. For them and me, the numbers were holy and sacred. Good or bad, I learned to play the ball where it lies when it comes to data.

In the end, I just put a positive spin on the subject of silver. It gave my readers one more chance to learn how to read another, different system.

My Final Thoughts

All my life, I have traveled to the beat of a different drummer. Not odd ball different, but different in in my way of thinking. As a kid, I was always trying to find a new way to do a boring job. My mom wanted me to mow the lawn in perfectly straight lines. For me, it was more fun to mow the lawn using smaller and smaller rectangles. I am not, never have been, and never will be a defender of the status quo.

It is high time for someone challenge the status quo when it comes to investing . Now is the time for an investing methodology that more accurately mirrors the technology of the realities of our time. It is a plain fact, computers are the dominant force in stock trading today. After all, you can't keep making the same mistakes over and over and expect any different results.

This book is the primer for something much bigger. It's a universe of hostile take overs and additions and deletions to the S&P 500. A place where universal buy and sell signals can be found. A new territory where you can determine the trend with a mere glance at two numbers. A land where you can make profits in bull and bear markets. The home of hyper over sold stocks. A means of controlling your future on the continents of the Dow 30, S&P 500 and the NASDAQ 100. My next book, Special Situations: The Winning Edge for Investors fulfills that vision.

Key to the Final Examination

1. T	41. D	81. D
2. F	42. U	82. D
3. b	43. D	83. D
4. F	44. D	84. D
5. F	45. D	85. D
6. T	46. U	86. D
7. b	47. T	87. D
8. F	48. T	88. D
9. F	49. T	89. D
10. T	50. F	90. D
11. T	51. D	91. D
12. F	52. D	92. U
13. T	53. D	93. U
14. F	54. D	94. D
15. d	55. D	95. D
16. T	56. D	96. D
17. T	57. D	97. D
18. T	58. D	98. D
19. F	59. D	99. U

20. T	60. D	100. c
21. F	61. D	
22. b	62. D	**Pop Quiz Key**
23. c	63. D	1. U
24. a	64. D	2. D
25. c	65. D	3. U
26. a	66. D	4. D
27. T	67. D	5. U
28. F	68. D	6. D
29. F	69. D	7. D
30. T	70. D	8. U
31. F	71. D	9. U
32. D	72. D	10. D
33. D	73. D	11. U
34. D	74. U	12. D
35. D	75. D	13. D
36. D	76. D	14. U
37. D	77. D	
38. U	78. D	
39. U	79. D	
40. D	80. D	

My standards are very high. If you scored better than 90%, you have a clear vision on the mechanics of the modern gold trading system. You have been liberated from the Old School mode of thinking. For you, buying an investment without regards to which system and how that system is performing is over and done.

REFERENCES

Ackerman, Kenneth D. The Gold Ring: Wall Street's Swindle of the Century and its Most Scandalous Black Friday, 1869. Carrol and Graff Publishers, New York, 2005.

Antilla, Susan. "Wall Street; A Fast-and-Loose Short Buster." The New York Times. August 12,1992.

The Arizona Republic. " What They're Buying." May 13, 2012, D-3.

Barnato, Katy. "Goldman Sachs Says It's Time to Short Gold." Yahoo! Finance. April 10, 2013.

Beattie, Andrew. "Closing Down the NYSE: What Does It Take?" Financial Edge, October 19, 2010.

Beattie, Andrew. "Silver Thursday: How Two Wealthy Traders Cornered the Market." Investopdia, July 8,2009.

Berthelsen, Christian, Shumsky, Tatyana, and Zackerman, Gregory. " Gold Sinks Into Bear Territory." WSJ, April 13, 2013, B-1.

Blumen, Robert. "Grantham Guarantees That Gold Will Crash." Gold's Daily Market Briefing, May 19,2000.

"Brady Report" Presidential Task Force on Market Mechanisms (1988).US Government Printing Office.

Burget, Philip. "CME Adding 10-oz. Gold Contract in October." Resource Investor. September 9,2010.

Burns, Katy, Day, Matt and Shumsky, Tatyana. " U.S. Probes Gold Pricing." WSJ, March 14, 2013, A-1.

CBS News. How Speed Traders are Changing Wall Street. CBSnews.com. October 11, 2010.

Cheng, Jonathan and Plever, Liam. "Gold at New High, $1,269.90." WSJ, September 18,2010, C-1.

Clarion Ledger.com. "Dr. Doom 2013 prediction: Nouriel Roubini's five reasons we're headed to a global recession." July, 2013.

Clark, DR. " A Stockbroker's Little White Lie: Are You Getting the Real Truth?" Yahoo! Finance, Contributor Network. April 18, 2011.

Cooper, Peter. " How Will Gold Perform As Interest Rates Rise?" Arabian Money, March 16, 2010.

Cui, Carolyn. " World is Bitten by the Gold Bug." WSJ, April22, 2011, A-1.

Day, Matt. " Gold Shoots Above $1,800: Fears of a Global Recession Spark Safe-Haven Buying, WSJ, August 19,2011, C-9.

Day, Matt. " A Wager of Metal's Silver Lining." WSJ, January 31, 2013, C-4.

DeMarche, Edmund. " 430 g coin-scam golden fleece." The New York Post. November 10,2010.

Domm, Patti. " No Shine: Gold Plunges Into Bear Market Territory." Yahoo! Finance. April 12, 2013.

Driebus, Terry L and Debaratl, Roy. " Gold falls most in 7 weeks as Comex margins rise." Bloomberg, August 11, 2011.

Dutram, Eric. " Has the Junior Gold Mining ETF Lost Its Luster?" Zacks. March 7,2012.

Garger, Kenneth. " Cocaine and Hookers for Wall Street Execs, Subsidized by You." The Fix. July 22, 2011.

Geraciotti, David. " Sex, Drugs and Financial Advisors." Wealth Management. Com. Sept. 24, 2010.

Hagenbaugh, Barbara. " Metals bolstered as dollar weakens." USA Today, January 6, 2004, B-1.

Hagenbaugh, Barbara and Krantz, Matt. " As dollar tarnishes, gold glitters, rising above $400 an ounce!" USA Today, December 2, 2003, B-1.

Hamlin, Jason. " Gold price manipulation exposed." Seeking Alpha, June 25,2010.

Hamilton, Adam CPA. "Real interest rates and the gold price." Commodities/Gold&Silver, December 5, 2008.

Hamilton, Paul. "Thinking Inside the Box: The Mind of Peter Lynch." unpublished paper, 2005.

Harding, Adella. " Gold prices dip to $418.90 Friday." Elko Daily Free Press, February 8,2005, A-3.

Johnson, John. "Short Sellers, False Rumors Under Scrutiny." newser. September 18,2008.

Johnson, Michael. " Gold ETF options for risk tolerant investors." Seeking Alpha, March 20,2011.

Krantz, Matt. " Gold rush could signal trouble." USA Today, May 10,2002, B-5

Krantz, Matt. " Nasdaq fined for bad Facebook IPO." USA Today. May 30, 2013.

Lewis, Al. "Taking it to the shorts, again." Market Watch. August 17, 2011.

Lutzenberger, Tim. "The history of gold commodities." eHow.com. November 27,2011.

Markham, Jon. " It's Time to Buy Gold Mining Stocks." Money Show. October 14,2011.

Mullins, Brody, Rothfeld, Michael, Mc Ginty, Tom, and Strasburg, Jenny. " Traders Pay for an Early Peek at Key Data." WSJ, June 13, 2013, A-1.

Neoclassical Economist. " Top 10 Most Shorted Gold Mining Stocks." Seeking Alpha. April 11,2012.

Moore, Michael. " Origins of gold ETF's." Gold Price, April 28, 2007.

Owles, Eric. "Wall Street's Race to the 48 Millisecond Trade." Yahoo! Finance. August 15, 2012.

Pilon, Mary; Pleven, Liam and Zweig, Jason. " Gold even reigns on stock market." WSJ, August 23,2011, C-1.

Pleven, Liam and Shumsky, Tatyana. " Gold sinks 5.6% as rally hits wall." WSJ, August 25,2011,C-1.

Prakash, Atul. " London Ritual Dating From 1919 Sets the Price of Gold." Reuters.com. Nov. 19, 2007.

Pulliam, Susan. "The World Does Not Need to End. A Gold Bull and His Prediction:$10,000 an Ounce." WSJ. October 30,2010.

Richards, Meg. " Experts remain divided on gold investing." Elko Daily Free Press, November 23,2004.. B-1.

Saefong, Myra P. and Kennedy, Simon. " Gold settles lower as inflation fears wane: Greek crisis, Bernanke comments prompt broad commodity decline." Market Watch, October 4,2011.

Shore, Sandy. " Gold prices plunge as economic fears ease for now." The Associated Press, August 24,2011.

Shumsky, Tatyana. "Inflation fears drive gold." WSJ. April 16, 2011.

Shumsky, Tatyana. " Gold climbs to above $1,400 as investors seek safe haven." WSJ, December 4,2010, B-13.

Shumsky, Tatyana. " CME raises Comex gold margin requirements." Market Watch, August 24, 2011.

Shumsky, Tatyana. " France downgrade fears lift gold." WSJ, August 10, 2011, C-5.

Shumsky, Tatyana. " Fed sends gold higher in after-hours trade." WSJ, August 10,2011, C-5.

Shumsky, Tatyana. " Silver Bears Pounce as Manufacturing Sputters." WSJ, April 3, 2013, C-1.

Smith, Aaron. "Weak dollar fuels the rise in gold and oil." CNN Money, October 5,2010.

Sullivan, Tom. " ETFs chasing pot of gold." Barron's, November 16,2009.

Strauss, Gary. " Bogus tweet is being probed: Hacked account led to Wall Street Panic." The Arizona Republic, April 25, 2013, D-1.

Stock, Kyle. "Wall Street Kicks Coke in Favor of Pot and Pills." Bull/Bear Report. August 20, 2013.

Tang, Frank. " Gold posts biggest drop since 1980 on Fed fears." Reuters, August 24,2011.

Task, Aaron. " After the Gold Rout: Blame Central Banks Manipulation, GATA's Powell." Yahoo! Finance, April 13, 2013.

Waggoner, John and Kirchoff, Sue. "Investors snap up gold as dollar sags." USA Today, Nov. 13,2002.

Waggoner, John. " While gold gets all the attention, silver goes on a run." USA Today, November 20, 2009, B-1.

Wikepedia. "Systems." Updated July 15, 2012.

Wikepedia. " Uptick rule." Updated December 12,2011.

Wilson, Lorimer. " Why Many Analysts See Gold as High as $10,000." Financial Sense. June 23,2010.

Whitakker, Matt. " Gold prices climb above $1,400, a first." WSJ, November 9,2010, C-12.

Zibel, Alan. " AP-CNBC Poll: Investors wary of stock trading." boston.com. September 14,2010.

www.ingramcontent.com/pod-product-compliance
Lightning Source LLC
Chambersburg PA
CBHW051324170526
45166CB00002B/670